DMITRI SHOSTAKOVICH

THE LIFE AND BACKGROUND
OF A SOVIET COMPOSER

DMITRI DMITRIEVICH SHOSTAKOVICH

Dmitri Shostakovich

THE LIFE
AND BACKGROUND
OF A
SOVIET COMPOSER

By *Victor Ilyich Seroff*

IN COLLABORATION WITH
NADEJDA GALLI–SHOHAT
AUNT OF THE COMPOSER

BOOKS FOR LIBRARIES PRESS
FREEPORT, NEW YORK

STANDARD BOOK NUMBER:
8369-5482-3

LIBRARY OF CONGRESS CATALOG CARD NUMBER:
73-126255

PRINTED IN THE UNITED STATES OF AMERICA

TO

Sophia Vassilievna Shostakovich

THE MOTHER
OF THE COMPOSER

───────────────────

*"Simply having children
does not make a mother."*

ACKNOWLEDGMENT

I WISH, first of all, to express my deep gratitude to my wife, Katherine, for her patient and invaluable help in the writing of this book.

My most sincere thanks go to Hermann Adler, Fritz Stiedry, Frank Black, Serge Koussevitzky, Olin Downes, Vladimir Bazykin, George Nebolsine, Artur Rodzinski, Simon Barer, Irving Deakin, Vladimir Drozdoff, Boris Brasol, William Dean Embree, Nicolas Slonimsky, Dr. Kenneth Taylor, Vladimir Lakond, Mr. and Mrs. George Gamov, Mrs. M. Oumoff-Malozemoff, Bruno Walter, and Sergei Rachmaninoff for the courtesy, the time, and the information they gave me.

I wish to acknowledge also the privileges extended to me by Mrs. Catherine Drinker Bowen, the Am-Rus Music Corporation, the American-Russian Institute, the *New York Times*, the *New York Herald Tribune*, the *New York World-Telegram*, the *New Masses*, the *Musical Quarterly*, *Vogue*, and the Slavonic Department of the New York Public Library.

V. S.

FOREWORD

It MAY appear to my readers that I have given an exceptionally detailed account of Shostakovich's family. The composer today is only thirty-seven; he has a long life of work and experience before him. When the time comes to record it in full, I believe his biographers will find much that is of value in this account of his family.

Ernest Newman writes: "In a first biography of any great artist a good deal that concerns his opinions of other people and his relations with other people has to be discreetly touched in with the lightest of strokes, if only because there are intimacies and susceptibilities on all sides to be considered."

I have taken the chance, for the sake of truth, of recording these "opinions" and "susceptibilities" where I feel the picture needs them.

"All first biographies," continues Newman, "should be written by some one with the entree to the inner circle of the subject — able consequently not only to extract illuminative reminiscences and avowals from the subject himself, but to tap, before it is too late, the memory of those who were intimate with him in the formative, early and middle periods of his life."

In gathering the material for this book, I have had to see a number of musicians, lawyers, economists, and statesmen, both of minor and of world fame. I am indebted to them for adding to my information.

FOREWORD

Sergei Rachmaninoff asked me whether I believed everything I was told by the men with whom I talked. I assured him that I have checked every statement; every fact in this story is backed by documents and material either in my possession or at the New York Public Library. I have even checked up on my collaborator, and it is my pleasure to compliment her on the accuracy of her memory.

V. S.

New York City
  December 14, 1942

ILLUSTRATIONS

DMITRI
SHOSTAKOVICH

THE LIFE AND BACKGROUND
OF A SOVIET COMPOSER

Chapter
1.

"One must BE something in order to DO something. Dante seems to us great; but he had the culture of centuries behind him. The house of Rothschild is rich; but it has taken more than one generation to accumulate such treasures. All these things lie deeper than is thought." — GOETHE

WHEN, on July 19, 1942, Dmitri Shostakovich's Seventh Symphony was heard for the first time in the Western Hemisphere, the name of the young composer was as familiar to Americans as those of Stalin and Timoshenko. Two months before this event Shostakovich's name was known for the most part only to musicians — and, at that, not to all of them. Today the "average" American can not only pronounce that name but even spell it. These people, to many of whom a symphony was merely a dull and heavy composition to be dialed off of their radios — these men and women were thoroughly aware of the importance of this particular symphony.

The story of the music was known to all before a note of it was played. The symphony was written, we were told, about the war — about the struggle of the Russian

3

people against the ruthless foe who destroyed their families and the peaceful way of their lives. It was composed under fire, in bomb-shelters; it was a composition dedicated to those who were willing to fight and to die for the freedom for which the United Nations were struggling.

The symphony was given its Russian "send-off" not merely with the recommendation of a competent music-critic, but, more importantly, with the widely publicized blessing of Russian war-heroes and popular writers whose names are well known throughout the Soviet Union. For the value of this composition to the Russian nation and to the morale of the Russian people at this time was fully realized by the Soviet government. The Russians, knowing the powerful influence of music on the people, also knew that there could be no better means of strengthening the ties between themselves and their Western allies. And so the symphony was given a tremendous advance "build-up."

Magazines and newspapers devoted columns to the young Russian composer, and page after page of photographs showed him walking with the citizens of Leningrad as a fire-warden during the siege. The transportation of his score was provided, not by a music agent, but by the governments of the United Nations and under their protection. And finally, public interest in America was keyed to a high pitch by the glamorous accounts of carrying the score on micro-film through Teheran to Cairo and by plane to New York.

There are vivid war-reports, there are letters about personal heroism, and moving-pictures showing a people's courage and despair — but nothing can surpass the direct emotional appeal of music. The whole drama of war and suffering can be broadcast over the air for all the world to hear and understand. For music is an international language of the imagination, with dimensions of fantasy that have no horizons.

The use of music as a power has been evident throughout history. Whenever the press and the free speech of a people were crushed by censorship, the national spirit found expression in music, either in lament or in revolt. The Russian revolutionary movement, which dates back several hundred years in its struggle against tyranny, built up a whole literature of "revolutionary" songs — songs strictly forbidden by the Czarist government. These songs were a powerful means of uniting the unhappy people and inspiring them to fight in spite of their suffering. Poland, Finland, all the small republics dreamt unceasingly of their national independence and expressed these dreams in their songs. But it will always rest with a symphonic composer to weld these folk-fragments into a powerful composition — one strong enough to ignite the imagination of an entire nation. For, as Aldous Huxley said in his essay on music, "We are incorrigibly civilized."

Dmitri Shostakovich's Seventh Symphony is superbly suited to being used as a piece of propaganda. Propaganda for foreign consumption must come as a creation of the immediate times, and its freshness is of great importance; it is most effective, as is all propaganda, when it deals with the vital needs of the man to whom it is directed. Shostakovich's Seventh Symphony is program music — that is, music portraying a definite story. This is something at which sophisticated musicians like to sneer, but it is in this story-portrayal that the power lies. A message expressed in this kind of music has great strength, for it appeals directly to the emotions and has nothing to do with the intelligence of the listener or the knowledge he possesses. It tells the man who hears it, not the story of a stranger, but his own story. It makes *him* the hero of it; it cries out his own sorrows and celebrates his own victories.

Shostakovich states that the beginning of the Seventh Symphony depicts the peaceful life before the war in the quiet homes of Leningrad. But to a listener in Iowa it could mean the meadow and the rolling hills around his home. After the fantastic theme of war, Shostakovich has put into his music a lament for the dead — and the tears of a Russian mother and of an American mother are the same.

The Seventh Symphony has fulfilled its political purpose, but time will show whether it can stand on its musical merit alone. It is evident that Shostakovich, mid-way in his "production period," has yet to solve the problem of welding his music into a compact symphonic form. In his Fifth, Sixth, and Seventh Symphonies, and even in his piano concerto, the first movements are by far the strongest and the best; only his First Symphony is uniformly evolved from the first note to the last. "Since the time of Haydn," says Bruno Walter, "the problem of a compact symphonic work, and particularly of its finale, has been a difficult one for all symphonic composers, including Beethoven."

The extent of the influence of different political and human philosophies on a composer is open to debate; but the most inspiring doctrine will not make a composer out of a man unless he is a musician. With the writing of his First Symphony, Shostakovich proved that here, without doubt, was a born composer — a man with a creative imagination and a thorough knowledge of his medium, an excellent craftsman with a language peculiarly his own. But to put a lofty political ideology into musical terms demands, in addition, a strong sense of the dramatic. A glance at the list of Shostakovich's compositions shows that half of them are written around dramatic subjects — operas, ballets, films. Add to this that Shostakovich at one time planned to devote ten years to composing an operatic tetralogy (of which *Lady Macbeth* was the beginning) — a task surpassing Wagner in the scope of its ambitions — and it becomes evident that Shostakovich is well equipped for his office of Soviet Composer.

The Russian people regard him today — as the Americans regarded Charles Lindbergh when he flew the Atlantic — as a national hero. He is the undisputed head of all musical enterprises, and has been elected an honorary member of the Leningrad Soviet; in April 1942, he took part in the Second Meeting of Slav Peoples in Moscow. Though most of his speeches, broadcast or sent to America as articles, appear to deal solely with music, they often reflect most clearly the intentions of the Kremlin.

The Soviet government proudly considers Shostakovich a product of Soviet culture; this is true as far as it goes, but it is less than half of what has made the man. The composer's intimate knowledge of his people's emotions and beliefs came not from any teaching, but from the history and traditions of his own family. "The tree of his moral culture," as Goethe has said, "had its roots in a wholly different soil." The roots of Shostakovich's creative power lie in his family background; the two generations before him were closely bound up with the events that built a new Russia.

The late Alexander Glazunov, speaking of Shostakovich, who was then in his twenties, said to Sergei Rachmaninoff: "To understand the mainspring of that boy's creative intellect, you must know that family — and particularly his mother."

* * *

Early on the morning of the 15th of April 1912 the world was awakened by the news of one of the greatest disasters in human history — the sinking of the S.S. *Titanic*. The troubles of Europe, which were inevitably leading to the first World War, were for a while almost forgotten. Little wonder that another tragedy, which took place two days later many thousands of miles east of the Atlantic, was hardly noticed though it was by far the more important in its significance.

The *New York World*, on Friday, April 19, 1912, carried this small paragraph on a back page:

HUNDRED GOLD MINERS SLAIN EIGHTY WOUNDED: SHOT DOWN NEAR IRKUTSK SI–BERIA, WICKEDEST CITY ON EARTH, BY RUS–SIAN TROOPS.

IRKUTSK, SIBERIA, April 18th: During a fight with Russian soldiers yesterday, 107 gold miners were killed and eighty were wounded. The outbreak occurred at the Lena Goldmining Company works, just outside the city, but the exact cause of the trouble is not known.

What actually happened was this: Two thousand miles north of Irkutsk, in the Siberian taiga, the workers of the Lena Gold Mine Fields, worn out by the inhuman conditions of living and labor, declared a strike on the 13th of March when they were served horse meat unfit to eat. In less than two weeks all the neighboring gold-field workers joined the strike and presented the administration of the Lena Gold Fields with the fourteen points of their demands.

These fourteen points illustrated the conditions under which six and a half thousand workers lived in this, one of the richest spots on earth. They demanded among other improvements an eight-hour working day instead of eleven and a half, the right to have one of their own representatives at the weighing of the gold, medical help, separate quarters for unmarried men and women, pay for overtime work, and the removal of certain officials whose cruel behavior they could stand no longer.

The strike was organized and carried through up to the 17th of April without violence, for the workers' committee for the strike took care that there was order, closed all the liquor stores for the duration of the strike, forbade gambling, and patrolled and guarded all explosives and inflammatory buildings. Special guards were placed at the dynamite stores. Negotiations were started with the heads of the company in St. Petersburg, but since these officials were willing to comply only with one or two of the demands, the situation remained at a deadlock.

Belozerov, director of the gold fields, called out the army and arrested all the representatives of the miners. Next morning, on that fatal April day, a mass of three thousand workers, unarmed, moved slowly across the fields toward the administration offices to demand from the officials the release of their deputies. The miners knew that these deputies would be considered independent agitators by the officials; therefore every man of the three thousand wrote his own petition stating his grievances, and carried it in his hand on the march across the fields.

They were met by an armed squad of two or three hundred soldiers, called in by Belozerov as reinforcements from Kirensk. The workers at the head of the procession, negotiating with the engineer and the commander of the squad, sat or stood quietly smoking cigarettes; but the crowd in the back, not knowing the reason for the delay, pressed increasingly up to the first lines. The officer, suddenly losing his nerve at the sight of the pushing mass of workers, ordered his men to shoot. How many were trampled down in the panic, besides the 270 killed and 250 wounded, no one knows, because the priest was not allowed to count them and they were buried together in one common pit.

This slaughter, regarded by Lenin as the turning-point in the spirit of the Russian Revolution, did not break the Lena strike, however, and three months later, in July, the workmen left the gold fields entirely.

Years later Dr. Nadejda Galli-Shohat, the aunt of Dmitri Shostakovich, talked of the Lena slaughter with a woman who had lived in the gold-mine region and to whom Nadejda was a stranger. This woman ended her story of the massacre with these words: "If Vassily Jakovlevich Kokaoulin had been alive, he would never have let this thing happen."

*   *   *

Vassily Jakovlevich Kokaoulin, grandfather of Dmitri Shostakovich, spent most of his life in a valiant endeavor to improve the inhuman living-conditions of the Siberian mine-workers. A native Siberian himself, born in Kirensk in 1850, he was well equipped to deal with life in that wild land, which does not give its wealth away without a bitter fight.

Only the steadily growing cities of Siberia are familiar to the outside world. The rest of the country — the taiga — is locked in silence by the snow and ice that have their grip on the land for nine months in the year. For centuries the men who sought fortunes there, together with peasants, runaways, political and common-law prisoners, had settled along the rivers, the only roads of communication. In Siberia there was only one rule of ethics — a man was never asked where he came from. It was nobody's business. "He came — that is all there is to the story. Perhaps he crawled out of a bear's den, for all you know." He came — and endured terrific cold, inhuman privation, and hard labor; he fought and died and others came, and only a few survived.

Those who survived, who were lucky enough to have built up a fortune by working and by fighting for it, by robbing and cheating in every transaction — these poured out their newly-gotten wealth in orgies that lasted for days, at which they ate and drank until they lost consciousness.

Even some of the so-called intellectuals, who, after serving their sentences for political crimes, were free to settle anywhere, were sucked into this life by the mad lack of restraint that surrounded them. Others of the settlers, who were not shrewd enough to profit by wild enterprise, in desperation joined the runaway convicts, "the incorrigibles," formed bands, and lived in the taiga. These bands held the settlers in mortal terror. They plundered and killed and even the Cossacks turned their backs and ran unless they were numerically superior, for the desperadoes were better armed and better shots. Much of their power they owed to the fact that they made and sold alcohol. Alcohol had, in Siberia, a value far greater than gold. For it was the chief protection from the cold and almost the only solace the men had for their bitter existence.

The mine-owners of the Lena Gold Fields recruited their workers from the Russian settlers, from convicts who had finished their term of hard labor, from runaways, from the thousands whom Fortune had ground under her heel and who called themselves Ivan Nepomnyashchi, meaning Ivan Who-Doesn't-Remember. From north, south, east, and west men streamed into the recruiting offices, lured by romantic stories of miners who stumbled over gold nuggets which meant fortune, freedom, and new life.

When they signed contracts, they signed their lives away. For the company gave them transportation money only at the end of the working year. If before that time a man was discharged or could no longer stand the work, he was left stranded in the middle of Siberia with no means of living or of getting anywhere.

Both Vassily Kokaoulin and his wife Alexandra felt that these were pioneering days and always considered themselves responsible for the welfare of the mine-workers. Alexandra Kokaoulin organized a school for the children of the miners, sent to St. Petersburg for the latest books and periodicals, and even started an orchestra of mine employees. She kept abreast of medical developments, and when the workers were skeptical of smallpox vaccination she had her son Jasha vaccinated first. She had a dominating personality and was more practical than her husband, Vassily; in fact, she was considered by the mine employees as the unofficial manager of the little settlement.

In all of Vassily's plans for the improvement of mine working-conditions he came up against the stubbornness and the greed of the Lena Gold Field officials in St. Petersburg. They did not want to spend money on modern equipment and were not interested in the lives of the miners. In reply to Kokaoulin's innumerable reports and letters the St. Petersburg administration would send an occasional official on a quick visit to the mines. This official would usually give a brief glance around, conduct a brisk and profitable purchase of furs, line his pockets with a little graft money, and return to St. Petersburg leaving Kokaoulin no better off than he was before.

Kokaoulin persevered, however, and during the ten years that he was manager of the gold fields he saw that at least a measure of justice was done his workers. He provided a pension plan for the employees, deducting a small percentage from each man's pay and, after a certain number of years' work, returning it to him as a pension. He was interested in some form of insurance for the workers since accidents were frequent and often fatal. Then came the idea of a new store where the workers could buy things cheaply. There was only one store in the settlement and the few goods for sale were priced very high. The new one would have a much larger stock and would operate on the principle of a Woolworth five-and-ten. Vassily also managed to put through the building of a narrow-gauge railroad along the twenty-five-mile stretch from Bodaybo to the mines themselves. He took no pay for this from the company although he could have collected a large sum.

Kokaoulin also did what little he could for the miners' physical welfare. The mines were worked in a primitive manner and the consequent bad ventilation and dangerous gases broke many a giant's health. The men worked all day in clothing soaked by the streams of water that ran constantly from the mine walls. When the Siberian night closed down, they emerged finally into air that was forty degrees below zero, and by the time they had covered the long distance home their clothes were frozen stiff with ice. They lived with their hungry families in unheated wooden barracks partitioned off like horse-stalls, and the unmarried men and women had no separate quarters. All the cooking was done over a huge bonfire outside. The cold inside was so intense that the miners' damp hair often froze as they slept.

Kokaoulin finally succeeded in having warm lockers

built near the mines where the men could change into dry clothes before the long trek to the barracks. But beyond this the Petersburg officials would not go, and up to the time of Kokaoulin's death the appalling physical hardships of the mine-workers remained unchanged. There was no law to protect them and their only defense was a solid comradeship with one another and the principle of "All for one, and one for all." They were fond of Kokaoulin, calling him "our father Kokaoulin," and they trusted him. When they surged out of the mines sometimes in angry revolt, Vassily had only to walk quietly among them to calm them instantly. For he was the only officer of the Lena gold mines — and the men knew it — who put no faith in the Cossack's whip.

Such were conditions in Bodaybo, where Vassily Kokaoulin married in 1871 and where his six children were born. To bring up a family in the way of honor, to guard them from cruelty and coarseness and disillusion in this atmosphere of greed and bitter drudgery, was truly an achievement.

*   *   *

The earliest memories of Dmitri Shostakovich's mother, Sophia (Sonya), were of the Bodaybo bridge spanning the turbulent little mountain river, yellow with sand carried down from the gold-washing; of the ancient gates leading to the entrance of the settlement, which stood always ajar as though someone, years ago, had forgotten to close them; of the wide square with its few wooden houses, built in a clearing over old mines that had been worked out and abandoned. It was a barren and depressing scene, but most of the time it was covered with a thick blanket of white snow and only for three months in the year did it show its ugly and unkempt face.

On some days the square was filled with Yakuts, the Siberian natives. They came to Bodaybo to trade or, in long caravans, to christen their children at the Russian Orthodox Church. Although they lived in nomadic tents and rubbed their faces with grease, some of the men possessed quite a fortune, particularly those who supplied the settlers with bear and antelope meat, fish, and furs. They wore voluminous sable coats, and hats two feet high. They had developed a strong taste for vodka and they sold everything from a fish to a new gold deposit for a bottle of it. They were attracted by the ritual of the christening and the festivities that followed and made much of the occasion; they gave away their sables and silver foxes in exchange for vodka, and when the time came to return home, they often got their newly christened children mixed.

Sonya was the third of the six Kokaoulin children, but she was the unquestioned commander of all their adventures. The stories of Jules Verne, *Robinson Crusoe, Uncle Tom's Cabin,* Walter Scott, all provided material for imaginative games, and Sonya always had the leading roles; she played the captains and the kings, she was Robinson Crusoe and she was also Topsy. She showed, already, traces of that dominant quality, inherited from her mother and so marked in the women of that family — a quality that was to carry her through the most desperate years of her life. She had a remarkable talent for mimicry, which stayed with her through childhood and developed later in life to an uncanny degree. She once went so far in her mockery of the priest who taught them at school that her mother had to punish her. Sonya had a keen intuitive judgment and had seen at once through the hypocrisy of the priest. But her mother was not deeply disturbed, for the Kokaoulins considered religion more as a tradition to be observed than as a spiritual necessity. They went to church only on important occasions such as Christmas and Easter, and the children were not forced to go at any other time.

The young Kokaoulins went to the school organized for the mine-workers' children. They lived in a large house provided by the mining company — a house staffed by fifteen servants. Alexandra, however, had brought her children up in the strict belief that this luxury might be only temporary and that the servants were not there to run at their bidding whenever they dropped a handkerchief. The company also detailed two armed Cossacks for their protection, but Kokaoulin did not believe in armed guards for himself or his family and firmly sent them back to their barracks. The servants were taken from among those who had been sent to Siberia for crimes and who had completed their sentences. Their past lives were a mystery and no one asked about them. The stewardess, they knew, had once been an equestrienne with a circus; the young groom who taught the children to ride had shot his superior officer, and the cook had been exiled to Siberia for life. Although no questions were asked, the crimes could usually be guessed from the punishments.

In 1890, at the age of twelve, Sonya entered the Irkutsk Institute for Noblewomen, founded by Nicholas I and open only to the daughters of the nobility and the privileged classes. There were only a few other schools in Russia as exclusive as the Irkutsk Institute. The school was housed in a huge building on an estate in the outskirts of Irkutsk, and strict discipline was maintained in fear of God and loyalty to the house of Romanov.

Sonya very quickly became accustomed to her new life. She was a brilliant student and the institute was proud of her. When Nicholas II, then the Crown Prince, came to visit the school, Sonya was presented to him by the Governor of Yakutsk. With two other girls, she danced for the future monarch the Mazurka from Glinka's opera, *Life for the Czar*. Sonya's musical education began here at the institute. Here she heard for the first time the classics of musical literature. She studied the piano, later conducted the church choir, and was soloist at all of the school concerts.

When the summer vacations began, Sonya went

home to Bodaybo with her brother Jasha, who was also studying in Irkutsk. She did not see very much of him during the winters for besides being six years older than she and already nearing his graduation, he kept to his own circle of friends. His interests lay in a radically different direction from those of his sister's school; his enthusiasms even then were for social reform and the revolutionary movement.

In 1896 Sonya graduated from her school with the highest honors given by the institute. She received the "Chiffre" award — the gold initials of the Czarina Alexandra Fyodorovna on a blue ribbon. This coveted ribbon — to be worn by the recipient on all important occasions — was the reward for great academic brilliance and assured a position as teacher to those receiving it who were in need of self-support. It was also a mark of distinction in the social world and gave the wearer the right to be presented at the court of the Czar.

After her graduation Sonya was the guest of honor at a magnificent ball given by the Governor General of Yakutsk. She had grown by this time into a young lady of beauty who carried herself proudly and she made a dazzling impression on the young officers at the ball.

*　　*　　*

In 1898 Vassily Kokaoulin decided to resign his position. The manipulations of the gold-field administration had become too involved for an honest, straightforward man. He had never taken undue advantage of his power as general manager as others did before and would do after him. Vassily's wife often urged him to declare his share of the mine profits, assuring his receiving a percentage of them. She said that he owed it to his children, but he stubbornly refused. "I do not want my children to be rich," he would say; "I want them to be educated."

Worries over the work into which he had put so much faith and hard labor had begun to tell on his health. He realized the futility of trying to convince the Petersburg officials that unless the plundering and speculation by the administration were stopped, unless the hit-or-miss methods of working the mines were replaced by scientifically sound methods, bankruptcy was inevitable. He had hoped that his eldest son would become a mining engineer, but Jasha had decided against it. Kokaoulin realized that the lives and future of his children lay in Russia proper and that they were all tired of Siberia and its nine months of cold. They dreamt of the sun of the Crimea, of palm trees, of warm winters, of fresh vegetables and fruit grown in their own gardens.

They decided to leave that same winter, waiting only for Kokaoulin to turn over his position to the new manager. Then the supplies were packed and the little caravan set out. They followed the frozen rivers in sleighs and made their way across untracked snow, marked only by the footprints of wild animals. At night they

21

slept well in the smoothly gliding sleighs, rocked to sleep by the bells on the harness of the horses, by the hiss of the runners and the lonely songs of the coach-men.

They arrived in Irkutsk around Easter and left the two younger sisters, Nadejda and Lyubochka, there to finish their schooling. Father, mother, and Sonya con-tinued their journey into Russia.

Often along the road they met groups of prisoners on their way to exile and hard labor. "The weary, ragged file of unshaven men dragged heavily clanking chains, fastened to their ankles and wrists," related Sonya. "They were herded by Cossacks on horseback and were followed by a lone *tilyega* [a flat open wagon], carrying the meager provisions and those of the con-demned who were too sick to walk. There were a few women in every group we met, but they walked un-chained."

At the stations along the way, the exiles were put into barred jails, called *ostrog.* These were sad encoun-ters for the Kokaoulins. While waiting for the horses to be changed they sometimes spoke to the prisoners, or sat quietly listening to their sad songs. These songs of the condemned stayed in Sonya's memory for the rest of her life.

Chapter
2.

IN September, after the family had completed a three months' pleasure trip on the Volga, they arrived in Moscow and Vassily and his wife decided to spend the winter in the Crimea. Nadejda succeeded in persuading her parents to let her enter the Bestuzhev College for Women in St. Petersburg. They were at first against it; their son Jasha, who was living in St. Petersburg, was active in the revolutionary movement and the Kokaoulins were afraid of his influence on Nadejda. They consented, however, when Sonya asked to remain with her sister and study music at the St. Petersburg Conservatory. They felt safe in leaving Nadejda with her level-headed sister.

In St. Petersburg, Nadejda was riding to her classes the first day in a hansom cab because she was late when, on the bridge over the Neva, she saw her brother Jasha walking slowly in the same direction. She jumped out of the cab, forgot her copy-books, lost her pencils — perhaps there was something in Vassily's premonitions.

When Jasha was still a boy on his high-school bench in Irkutsk, he had begun to be interested in social reform. Most of his classmates were the sons of exiled revolutionists, and the grandsons of the Dekabrists. With them, Jasha studied Marx, Plekhanov, Engels, and read the much-disputed works of Tolstoy and Dostoyevsky. When he came to St. Petersburg, therefore, he was ripe and well equipped theoretically for the revolutionary movement. He remained at the university in Petersburg for an unusually long time — some eight years. This was partly due to the fact that at first he wasted a great deal of his time, as did many a young man who had come from the depths of the provinces to the dazzling life of the capital. His father provided him with ample means to enjoy his youth and his new life. His long stay at the university was also partly on account of his revolutionary activities, for they took up a great deal of his class-time. Capital, regardless of its amount, was always most welcome in revolutionary circles and Jasha was never, in this respect, merely a bystander. His inherited generosity and good comradeship — *rubakha paren* — were not the only traits that made him popular among the students. His erudition, his sober judgment, and his humor were his outstanding qualities. Although he loved music, his favorite composition being Beethoven's Ninth Symphony, and knew the Petersburg art gallery, the Hermitage, backwards and forwards, he was very scornful of his sisters who studied music and science instead of being professional revolutionists. But the chief reason for his spending eight years at the university was that he was a brilliant student and, since his father provided him with his means of living, he saw no particular hurry in becoming independent.

To be near her sister's dormitory, Sonya took a room with a family by the name of Gamboyev, who lived only a short distance from the university. She had known the Gamboyev girls in the Irkutsk Institute. They were native Siberians and their father held a prominent position as representative of the Russian government in Peking, China. The mother with her three daughters and two sons lived in St. Petersburg on a rather lavish scale. The boys, who were still students, were excellent dancers and loved music. The house was always full of young people and in the evenings Sonya played the piano, either accompanying the son, Volodia, who played the violin, or playing the new dances that were being introduced that year — the vingerka, the pas-de-quatre, the pas-d'Espagne, and the chaconne.

Jasha came often to the Gamboyevs' to see his sisters and one evening, after they had all been singing together, he declared: "Ah, but wait, I will bring around a young fellow. Just wait till you hear Mitya sing!" A few nights later he brought to the house a young man whom he had known in Irkutsk and who had gone to the same high school — Dmitri Boleslavovich Shosta-kovich.[1] Dmitri was about five feet five, rather stocky, with light brown hair, a light mustache and a pair of very gay dark eyes. The two young men brought piles of music with them and that evening after tea Dmitri sang for the Gamboyevs' guests. Sonya accompanied him at the piano. He was obviously very happy to show off his voice, and he sang with ease and very musically, arias from Tchaikovsky's operas as well as popular romances. He had a tenor voice and, though not trained, he knew how to use it. After this visit Dmitri came very often and it was obvious that he came on account of Sonya.

The following three years the sisters spent in St. Petersburg, Nadejda at the university and Sonya at the conservatory. Sonya entered first the piano class of Mme Malazemova, who was considered by some as good a teacher as the famous Mme Essipov, although she was of a different school. Mme Essipov was the wife and pupil of Leschetizky, while Mme Malazemova belonged to that group of adoring Petersburg ladies to whom Anton Rubinstein was the undisputed god of the piano. But Mme Malazemova conducted an advanced class for which Sonya was not yet ready and it was suggested that Sonya work with her assistant, Mme Rozanova.

Jasha and his sisters received an ample income from their father, and the girls were dressed by the finest

---

[1] See "The Shostakovich Family" in Appendix.

dressmakers in the capital. Jasha, however, spent all his money on his revolutionary friends and lived very modestly. Dmitri, who was studying histology at the university, accompanied Sonya everywhere. The young people went to every concert and opera and had their best time waiting in the long queues for tickets for the gallery, for such was the tradition of the Russian students of the day.

In February 1899, serious disturbances broke out in St. Petersburg. These started with a demonstration by the students on Kazan Square demanding freedom of speech, of assembly, and of worship, the separation of the government from the church, and, finally, a constitutional government. As soon as the demonstrations had gained momentum, the Cossacks were ordered out to disperse them. They rode into the crowd of students, lashing out with their nagaikas (short Cossack whips). The students who fought back were arrested, along with those who had been spied on and denounced.

All of the institutions of higher education joined the students and declared a strike. Nadejda's college joined with the rest and was the central meeting-place for the students in their protests against the Cossack treatment. Both sisters were very worried about Jasha, and about Dmitri and the Gamboyev boys. A student's cap, in those days, was enough to get its wearer arrested as he walked along the street. It was one thing to be a part of the resplendent institute in Irkutsk which glorified the Romanov family, a part of the ceremonies and the splendid balls, to prefer the elegant officers to Jasha's proletarian friends; but these values changed when Cossacks trampled under their horses' feet, and slashed with their nagaikas, the faces of students who might have been Jasha or Dmitri or the Gamboyevs.

The two sisters did not at once join the ranks of the revolutionists, but their sympathies with the students were apparent. They attended every student ball and party, and though these parties had an innocent surface of youthful revelry, in reality they were the meeting-places for the revolutionary youth of all Russia. The first of such balls had been organized by the Siberian Zemstvo with the idea of helping the financially poor Siberian students. But the money was completely in the hands of the students and, this league being definitely a revolutionary organization, part of the proceeds always went to the cause.

Sonya was in the full bloom of her beauty, with a mass of chestnut hair and serious dark green eyes. Brilliantly educated, with unbounded fantasy and good taste, and an able musician, she did a great deal toward making those evenings a success.

In the winter of 1901 Sonya was a frequent visitor at the home of a man who had been her tutor in Bodaybo, Alexander Beklemyshev. His brother was the famous sculptor whose statue of Tchaikovsky still stands in the Leningrad Conservatory of Music. It was here that she met the famous singer Fyodor Chaliapin, and accompanied him on the piano when he sang that evening. This experience made a lasting impression on Sonya, for Chaliapin was the first great musician whom she met. He talked at great length to her about the importance of hard and concentrated work in every art. Sonya remembered every word of what he said and in later years repeated it often to her children.

That winter Sonya found the Gamboyev house too gay and noisy for her work, and she and Nadejda went to live with Clavdia Lukashevich, the famous writer of children's stories.

"From then on," said Nadejda, "I worked out all my mathematical problems to the accompaniment of Chopin études, Beethoven sonatas, and the trios that were played every evening. Even today, when I hear a fragment out of a classical piece, it brings back to me the memory of my room and of a particular problem connected with that music."

One evening in the early spring of 1902 Sonya came home with exciting news for Nadejda. "I met Dmitri Shostakovich as I was coming from the conservatory," she said to her sister. "We went for a ride on the Isles and he asked me to marry him." Sonya and Nadejda talked the whole night through of the future and of what they were going to do. Sonya would continue her music and Nadejda would live with them, since she had only one more year at the college. They decided not to say anything to their parents until summer, when Dmitri would spend his vacation with them on the small estate in Alushta, on the Black Sea, which

Vassily Kokaoulin had bought the year before. Sonya was worried about how her mother would take the news. To Russian ears Shostakovich was a Polish-sounding name and she knew that, true to Russian tradition, her mother felt strongly about the Poles.

Dmitri got along well with the Kokaoulins, however, and when the sisters returned to St. Petersburg in the autumn, Sonya was officially engaged.

On the 31st of January 1903 [2] Sonya and Dmitri Shostakovich were married in Alushta, with only the family present.

*   *   *

In October 1903 Sonya's first child was born. It was a girl, whom they called Marusia. Sonya stopped her work at the conservatory altogether and from then on was occupied only with her home. Dmitri held a position as chargé d'affaires at the Petersburg Chamber of Weights and Measures; [3] his salary was only a hundred rubles a month and the small family had to live very modestly. Until her marriage Sonya had not known the meaning of need. She had spent her young life in comparative luxury, graduated from one of the best schools in Russia, which had given her good social standing — and then had fallen in love and married a man who had little money and who was only at the beginning of his career. From the little daredevil who lived in her dreams

---

2 Dates in this volume are according to the Julian Calendar (Old Style) up to February 1, 1918, when it was supplanted in the USSR by the Gregorian Calendar (New Style), the one in general use.

3 Similar to the United States Bureau of Standards.

in Bodaybo, from the young beauty who turned the heads of students and officers, Sonya had matured into womanhood with a will and a determination equaled only by her own mother's. She wanted now, above all things, the happiness of married life.

In February 1904 the Russo-Japanese War broke out. Dmitri, having been born in Narim, Siberia, of exiled parents, was exempt from military service, for the government did not trust these men and would not draft them into the army. The life of the little family was filled with anxiety none the less. By 1905 the nominal wages of workers had fallen and at the same time the war had caused prices to rise. The basic necessities of meat and bread were lacking and the country was restless with revolt. The state of the workers grew steadily worse; exhausted by labor, raddled with vodka, disease, and hunger, living in filth and misery, with no civil rights whatever and no assurance of steady work — since corruption and bribery ruled the choice of employees — they were fertile soil for any scheme that might better their lot.

Dmitri was not a revolutionary, but the mere fact that his family lived in St. Petersburg and belonged to the intellectual class which was so interested in the social movement, added to the fact that a great many of their friends were revolutionists, brought daily uncertainty into their lives. There was hardly a home or a family that was not involved in the revolutionary idea. Jasha, who was always considered the "Red" in the

Kokaoulin family, had discovered after his graduation from the university that he could not agree with his reactionary superior in the Petersburg Chamber of Weights and Measures and had moved to Rostov, far from any political excitement. But Dmitri's own brother-in-law, Maxim Kostrykin, was an ardent revolutionist who had been exiled to Siberia and had returned under a false passport, and Sonya's youngest sister Lyubochka, who had just graduated from high school and entered the university, was deeply involved in the movement. These two and their friends brought daily news and discussions into the Shostakovich household, and this alone was enough to make Sonya and Dmitri sympathizers, almost accomplices in the eyes of the government.

The ominous tragedy that took place in St. Petersburg at the beginning of 1905 made more revolutionists out of people who formerly had been in no way concerned with the movement than any teaching of revolutionary theories could have done. A young priest, Gregory Gapon, had won the confidence of thousands of workers in St. Petersburg. The thirty-five-year-old Gapon was a fantastic and complex figure — a combination of hysterical enthusiast, adventurer, and impostor. The workers, knowing how ruthlessly every strike and revolt was punished, were apt to shy away from the professional revolutionist; but Gapon had been living among them and had told them that he believed the Czar was the loving father of his people.

Gapon promised that he would lead them before the Emperor of all the Russias and make him "receive the workmen's petition into his own hand."

Carrying ikons, crosses, church banners, and pictures of Nicholas, and headed by Gregory Gapon dressed in his priest's robes, several thousand workmen came peaceably to the Winter Palace on January 9 to present their petition. They were joined on the way by the students and intellectuals of all Petersburg, and by hundreds of spectators. They expected that their Czar Nicholas would come out on the balcony of the Palace. They did not know that several hours before, Nicholas, learning of the march, had left Petersburg and gone to Tsarskoe Selo.

Instead, they were met with volleys from the guns of Uhlans, Cossacks, and guards, which killed and wounded several thousand men and put an end to this romantic revolutionary adventure. It put an end also to liberal ideology and tactics, which were based on the assumption that the Russian people were not ripe for revolution.

A wave of hatred and revolutionary determination among the masses marked the beginning of widespread uprisings. "Victory demands not a romantic method but a revolutionary one," cried the leaders of the parties, and their ranks were swelled with new thousands who were not going to beg but to demand and fight. When it was discovered later that Gregory Gapon had played the double role of friend of labor and agent of the police, the indignation against the government rose to a dangerous pitch.

Nadejda, who had married and had been living in Moscow for two years, came to St. Petersburg at this time to work in the Institute of Physics and lived with the Shostakoviches. Dmitri, his brother-in-law, and many of their friends had been that fatal day in front of the Winter Palace and the talk among them was only of that Bloody Sunday and the events that followed it. Nadejda's own colleagues at the institute were deeply involved; both students and professors sided with the workmen.

Nadejda herself was quickly swept into the spirit of her surroundings and became a member of the Social Democratic Bolshevik Party. She was assigned the task of mimeographing the propaganda pamphlets, proclamations, and other matter. This was delicate and difficult work, for there was as yet no mimeographing machine and she had to set her own type in wax. She also used a typewriter which her brother-in-law Dmitri lent her. Though she was very serious in her studies and frankly upset by the interruptions that the political disturbances caused, sometimes keeping her away from the institute for many weeks, she spent a great deal of time attending student meetings as well as those of her own party.

During that year Nadejda did all her mimeographing in her room at the Shostakovich home. Students and workmen brought her the material and took it away when it was finished, and Nadejda never knew where it went. These students, and the workmen, who were themselves dressed as students, had party names and addressed Nadejda always by her party name. She was aware of the fact that her illegal occupation was spied upon and as she went home from her meetings she felt more than once that she was being followed. She used to try to get rid of her followers by slipping off of the trolley-cars unseen or by taking a different route to her home. At home, when she was through with her work, she would put the typewriter with all the material into the stove — a naïve place to choose for safety from the police!

In her room at the laboratory, where she was working as a physicist, she kept in safety the code and all the more valuable material which was brought to her. All this work was done under the constant fear that at any time the apartment might be ransacked by the police, with very grave consequences, not only for Nadejda but for the whole Shostakovich family.

But luck was with them, and when the police finally did come to search the house, the typewriter was in Moscow with all the literature and the code, and Nadejda was sitting in her parents' garden enjoying the Crimean sun and completely submerged in higher mathematics. Sonya was away with her baby in the country near St. Petersburg.

It was Dmitri who, coming home from work, found the door to his apartment open and all the lights on as if for a party. He was met in the vestibule by two policemen in civilian clothes, who ordered him to turn out his pockets and then searched him from head to foot. They demanded the keys to the chest of drawers and to the closets, and while they were going through his mail and his personal belongings, he saw the janitor talking earnestly to a policeman in the next room. The police took all of his mail and a few books that looked to them like suspicious literature, and left.

This material and Dmitri's papers were taken to the Okhranka for examination. The Okhranka (the Russian secret-police organization) already had a record of the revolutionary activities of Jasha, who had once had to flee from arrest as far as Bodaybo; they might still find out that Nadejda was a member of the Bolshevik Party — and Dmitri himself was the son of a political exile.

From that time on, Dmitri and Sonya lived under strain and in uneasiness, for the suspicions of the Okhranka might result in arrest at any moment.

*   *   *

In the fall of 1906 Sonya was expecting her second child. During the two years that had passed since the birth of Marusia, Sonya had begun to fear that she was not going to have any more children and so in September she awaited this second birth with joy. She decided to have her child in her own home on Nikolaevskaya Street, with only a midwife in attendance, a tall,

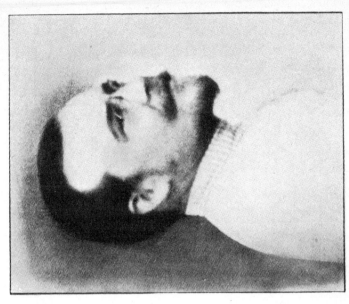

Dmitri Boleslavovich Shostakovich (1902), father
of the composer.

Vassily Jakovlevich Kokaoulin, grandfather of the
composer (taken in 1902).

brawny woman who shocked both Sonya and Nadejda with her jovial language and her offhand, matter-of-fact manner.

The child was born at five o'clock on the afternoon of the 12th of September [4] 1906 — a fine, healthy boy.

The day of his christening was a busy one in the Shostakovich household. His father, Dmitri, had come home early from work loaded down with packages of delicacies for the celebration. The whole house was in a busy turmoil. A room had to be prepared for the baptism and the dining-room arranged for the tea. The baby slept peacefully in his crib, oblivious of the excitement and gaiety that surrounded him. His three-year-old sister, Marusia, ran about under everyone's feet, eager to participate and to miss nothing. At three o'clock the priest and his attendant arrived, the font was placed in the middle of Dmitri's study, and the family gathered for the ceremony.

"What name do you want to give to your boy?" the priest asked the parents. "We want to call him Jaroslav," they replied. The priest raised his eyes in astonishment. "That is a very unusual name," he said. "You wouldn't know what nickname to give him, and his friends in school wouldn't know what to call him. No, no, that name will not do."

The family looked at each other, smiling a little, not understanding the priest's objection to the chosen name.

---

[4] According to the old Roman calendar; September 25, New Style.

"Why don't you call him Dmitri?" continued the priest; "it is a good Russian name and his father's name too."

"But," said Sonya, "Jaroslav Dmitrievich sounds much better than Dmitri Dmitrievich."

But the priest waved aside her objections. "Dmitri is a good name," he said; "we'll call him Dmitri." So the matter was settled.

According to Russian Orthodox custom, the parents are not allowed to be present at the actual ceremony. The child was attended by its godparents. "You be careful," said Sonya worriedly as she handed her son to his godfather; "don't drop him, and make sure the water is not too cold." The doors to the study were closed and the family stayed outside, hearing snatches of the ceremony within.

"Do you renounce the devil and all his works?"

"We do renounce the devil and all his works."

"Do you believe in God, the Father Almighty, Creator of heaven and earth?"

"We do believe."

This was repeated several times; then the priest recited the credo; there was the sound of splashing water and suddenly the lusty yells of little Mitya. The doors were flung open and the happy parents received their child, who was immediately taken back to his crib. The priest did not stay for the tea, and as soon as he had left, Lyubochka wanted to know why he had objected so strenuously to the name Jaroslav. "He probably did not know which is the date for the name-day of Saint Jaroslav," said the godfather. "Dmitri he was sure of."

The family celebrated with a long and lavish meal at which many toasts were drunk; afterwards they sang and played duets until late in the evening.

Chapter
3.

THREE months of happiness passed for the Shostakovich family. Every day when Dmitri came home from his work, he would go straight to his son's room and play with him. It was he who dressed little Mitya and took care of him at night. As he did this, he laughed and sang to his son and talked to him as he used to talk to his playmates in Irkutsk.

Mitya's father was endowed with singularly good health; he woke up every morning with a smile and possessed an unshakable optimism and a contagious good humor. The nurse, Sasha, used to say: "The master wakes up like a baby; as soon as he opens his eyes he begins to laugh and talk." He always rose before the rest of the family had awakened, and went about his early morning tasks singing, teasing the cook, and joking with the nurse. Sonya blossomed under the warmth of her family life, and the only thought that marred her perfect happiness was that her mother could no longer share it with her. Alexandra Kokaoulin had died in Alushta the previous March.

The revolutionary storm had passed over their heads without striking any member of the family; but they were not to have peace for long. On New Year's Eve of 1906 the fiancé of Sonya's young sister Lyubochka, Vyacheslav Yanovitsky, was arrested in a police raid on a student's apartment in St. Petersburg — a raid in which one policeman was killed and three others wounded. Yanovitsky, who was a brilliant student at the Institute of Technology, was known to be an active member of the Social Revolutionary Party and the situation was grave, for the police report stated that the accused students were to be tried by court martial. At the time of Yanovitsky's arrest, these court martials were orgies of punishment; sometimes in one week a hundred and fifty people were hanged in St. Petersburg alone. The new Minister of the Interior, Stolypin, was engaged in stamping out all traces of revolutionary activity with brutal and ruthless thoroughness. These wholesale hangings gave to the current administration the nickname of "Stolypin's Necktie." Thousands of people were arrested throughout Russia and brought to court, where they were judged by army men, most of whom had had no judicial education or experience. There were only two possible verdicts — the noose or freedom — and decisions were handed down by the courts within twenty-four hours after arrest with little or no investigation.

Voronov, the head of the Institute of Technology, asked the Minister of Education to intercede on behalf

of the students, and was able to report to the Shostakovich family a few days later that all danger of immediate trial by court martial had been removed. He
impressed upon them the importance of getting the
public opinion of the Petersburg intelligentsia on the
side of the students, as well as the support of prominent members of society and of the professions. Sonya
realized that this vital work was up to her. Stolypin's
attitude toward students in general was one of hostile
suspicion and therefore both Nadejda and Lyubochka
could do Yanovitsky the most good by keeping as far
in the background as possible.

Sonya knew that there was a case of murder staring
them in the face. The killing of human beings, the
destruction of human liberties and homes, which bring
a shudder of repulsion in peaceful times, become during a war heroic deeds. Patriotism cancels out the
criminality of these acts and rewards them with praise.
Revolution is very similar to war in this respect and
makes the committer of the crime a martyr to his cause
and a romantic figure, since he is willing to risk his liberty and his life. The government's exceptionally cruel
punishment, and the significance given the act by the
intellectual class, put an aura of heroism over it. But
one does not debate the rights and wrongs of revolution when it strikes in one's own home and Sonya realized how much Yanovitsky would have against him at
his trial. And this affair was dangerous not only to her
young sister but also to her own home, for it was hardly

eighteen months ago that her house had been ransacked by the police and her husband's papers filed in the records of the Okhranka.

She was far more aware of all the dangers involved in the student movement than were her sisters, who loved the romantic excitement of it, and they had complete faith in her ability to guide the family through this disaster. Sonya had always held herself apart from all political activities; her past record was impeccable enough for the most reactionary of officials. She had poise and good looks, the social standing that she had gained by her brilliant education at the Romanov Institute, and, in winning the award at Irkutsk, the right to be presented at the court of the Czar. There was not a home or an office in St. Petersburg that would be closed to her, and no official would dare not to listen to her with attention.

She went to see the vice-president of the St. Petersburg Lawyers' Association, Michael V. Bernshtam, a man respected in the city both by his colleagues and by the government. Through his influence Russia's most famous lawyer, Oscar Grusenberg,[1] volunteered to take Yanovitsky's case free of charge. For a long time Grusenberg was consistently denied a report of the investigation, which was in the hands of the Military Department of Extraordinary Affairs; but Bernshtam brought

---

[1] Oscar Grusenberg's name became known even in America through his defense of Beilis in the famous "Ritual Murder Trial" which took place in Kiev in 1913.

his influence to bear upon the press. The editorials were strongly in favor of the students, and public interest in the case was not allowed to flag for an instant. Lyubochka, who had finally been permitted by the prison authorities to see her fiancé, brought back to Sonya Yanovitsky's statement that the affair had started merely as an innocent New Year's Eve party and that he himself had neither carried a gun nor fired one. Sonya pursued her task with renewed energy and faith, for she had known Yanovitsky a long time and was convinced that he was not a man who would put the blame for his actions on the shoulders of another.

The long month of January dragged by. The Shostakovich family lived in misery and tension. Lyubochka bore up with remarkable stoicism; Sonya was away from the house most of the time, seeing everyone she could who was connected with the case. She had little time for her baby son; she only returned home to him at feeding-time, for she was still nursing him. She left him in the care of Lyubochka, who was happy to have something to occupy her worried thoughts.

In February Lyubochka decided to marry Yanovitsky in prison as soon as permission could be obtained. For if the best should happen in the military court and he should be freed, there was the possibility of his immediate re-arrest by the police if the slightest revolution· ary activity out of his past could be dug up and proved at his first trial. Exile for life was not an unusual out· come of a political trial with no murder involved. Lyubochka knew that only wives were allowed to follow political prisoners into exile and she made up her mind to take no chances. Old Vassily Kokaoulin came to St. Petersburg and on the 19th of February, in the home on Nikolaevskaya Street, Lyubochka, dressed in a white wedding-gown and carrying a bouquet of white cyclamen as though she were to be married in a great cathedral, was blessed by her father and Sonya and presented with bread and salt, according to old Russian tradition. Their friends had remembered the little bride on her wedding-day and the house was filled with flowers; before she left, her father put a ten-ruble gold piece in her shoe, signifying that she would walk in wealth all her married life.

Sonya and Dmitri drove her to the Kresti prison, where Yanovitsky was held. Unlike other prisons, the Kresti was composed of single cells and every prisoner was kept alone. This grim building had broken the health and morale of more than one man, and its supreme privacy had driven many a noble spirit to insanity.

The simple ceremony was quickly performed, with the young bride and groom surrounded by heavily armed guards. Yanovitsky was pale and his blue eyes were haggard, but he carried himself proudly, as befitted the son of an old and aristocratic Polish family. Dmitri was deeply moved by the sorrowful wedding, for it brought before his mind a picture of his own parents. His mother, too, had been ready to follow her exiled husband wherever he was sent. He himself was now a part of the drama that had involved so many whose tragic stories he had heard in his youth in Narim.

Another week of anxiety passed, but the prosecutor still did not set a date for the trial. It was an old trick in Russian courts to delay the hearing of a political prisoner and, by holding him for a long time in suspense, to break his morale. In Yanovitsky's case the delay was also partly due to the prosecutor's hope that eventually the popular clamor would die down and the press would relax its interest.

The court finally issued an official statement that the Yanovitsky trial would be held on the 7th of March 1907, at twelve o'clock. The tension in the Shostakovich household grew and the members of the family held closely together and bolstered each other's spirits as well as they could. Lyubochka was counting, not the days, but the hours. .

At last the 7th of March arrived. The building in which Yanovitsky's trial was held was guarded as though under siege. The surrounding streets as well as the courtyard looked more like a military camp than a palace of justice. Scores of extra police were placed on duty at every entrance.

Sonya and Dmitri pushed their way into the packed courtroom and promptly at twelve o'clock the trial began. Headed by the prosecutor, four colonels of the Czar's Guard in full regalia entered and took their places at the table. Grusenberg and his two colleagues followed, dressed in black frock-coats, with the small silver insignia of their profession on their lapels. Then the three accused students, pale and haggard, were brought in by armed guards with unsheathed sabers over their shoulders, and, the preliminary formalities having been gone through, the complete indictment was read to the courtroom and the questioning ensued.

Yanovitsky was the first to be called. The evidence against him consisted entirely of the vague recollections of the police who were at the scene. One policeman insisted that the man who shot and killed his fellow officer had a cut eye. Yanovitsky himself had a cut over one eye, but he testified that this was the result of the beating he had received from the police when they arrested him. The prosecution then pointed out that during the raid of December 31 two students had fled down the stairs, firing over their shoulders as they ran. The accused Yanovitsky maintained that he was not one of them, yet his coat had been found in the courtyard where the fleeing student, Surba, had shot himself. Yanovitsky replied that during the firing Surba had leaped for the door and grabbed up his, Yanovitsky's, coat by mistake. The two students accused with Yanovitsky followed him on the stand, and the court then started its examination of the witnesses for the defense — students, professors, workers, men of letters. They spoke of Yanovitsky as a man of calm nature and clear reasoning, incapable of violence; they pointed out that he had been for several years the president of his student society, and that his influence had more than once kept the students from violent outbreaks.

On the second day of the trial Grusenberg called Sonya to the stand as his chief witness. Dressed in fashionable clothes, with a silver-fox fur over her shoulders, Sonya took her place with quiet poise and confidence. Grusenberg asked her to tell the court of Yanovitsky's relations with the Shostakovich family, and as Sonya described in simple words her sister's love for this man and her marriage to him in the chapel of the Kresti, the court listened in a silence broken only by an occasional sob among the spectators.

When Grusenberg's colleagues had finished their summing up on behalf of Yanovitsky's two fellow students, Grusenberg himself rose for the closing speech. "For sixty-seven days the noose has hung above the heads of these three accused." Thus Grusenberg began his speech in defense of Yanovitsky — a speech that is known and remembered to this day.

*   *   *

Late on that evening of March 8 the court was still in session. The debate raged furiously, and finally at eight o'clock the judges retired and deliberated for two hours. When they returned to take their places, the crowded courtroom was so silent and tense that the footsteps of the judges sounded like the beat of hammers. When they had taken their places, the president of the court turned to the defendants and called out:

"Sukhleyev!" The first student rose and faced the judges indifferently. "Accused, you are innocent. Shishkin!" The second student, a nineteen-year-old boy, stood and turned his childlike face to the prosecutor. "Accused, you are innocent. Yanovitsky!" called the prosecutor. Yanovitsky rose, pale but proudly erect; a quiver went through the crowd, and it seemed as though all breathing had stopped. "Accused, you are innocent."

Wild cheers broke out in the courtroom. Someone fainted and the sobs of women could be heard. The crowd rushed forward to congratulate the lawyers, the judges shook the hands of the three free men, caps were thrown in the air, and even the policemen were embraced and slapped on the back. Yanovitsky was taken by Dmitri and a weary but triumphant Sonya back to the Shostakovich home, where his wife and his mother were waiting for him.

For the rest of her life, on every 8th of March Lyubochka sent a telegram of gratitude to Grusenberg.

Chapter
4.

GRADUALLY life in the Shostakovich family resumed its normal course. Father Vassily lived with Sonya, and Dmitri soon took up a new position in the office of the estate of Adolf Romanovich Rennenkampf. This huge estate was located within two hours of St. Petersburg. The peat industry on the estate was the chief source of Rennenkampf's wealth. It was undoubtedly through Sonya that her husband obtained the position, for Rennenkampf's wife was an old friend of hers.

At first Dmitri combined his duties on the estate with the position he held at the Chamber of Weights and Measures, but before long Rennenkampf appointed him general manager and he gave up his other work for his new duties. There was a large house on the estate which Rennenkampf turned over to the Shostakoviches and this became their summer residence. Rennenkampf was never there in the summer and so the family had the free run of the estate.

The summer of 1908 they spent not far away in
Viborg, in Finland. Here, on the 8th of August, Sonya
had her third child. Both she and Dmitri were so convinced that it would be a boy that when Dmitri came
to see his wife in the hospital, he referred constantly to
"him." At first Sonya thought he was joking, but finally
she told him that he had a daughter. Dmitri realized
that he had already told Father Vassily that the child
was a boy and that by this time Vassily, as had been his
custom for the last eight years, must have sent tele-
grams to that effect to all the rest of the family. Dmitri
immediately corrected his mistake and Vassily had to
send out a second message. From all parts of Russia
answers came from the members of the family, advis-
ing Sonya to make sure the hospital had given her the
right baby and saying that it sounded to them like a
Yakut christening in Bodaybo. Both Sonya and Dmitri
looked anxiously into the baby's face from time to
time for signs of family resemblance.

As soon as Sonya was up, they took the train for St.
Petersburg. To the stern customs official at the border,
the nurse said: "This is all we have to declare. We acquired this in Finland."

They called their third child Zoya, the Greek word
for "life."

When the Shostakoviches returned with their new
baby, Vassily went to live with Lyubochka and her husband, who had returned to St. Petersburg. Yanovitsky
had to serve his year of military duty, and Lyubochka

was happy to have her father with her. She was not well. Her health had begun to show the results of the strain she was under during Yanovitsky's imprisonment; the first signs of tuberculosis appeared. It was during the year that Vassily lived with her that Lyubochka learned to love and admire in him the man he was and the father that she had scarcely known as a child.

He gave her great moral support during the three difficult years after their return. He was, besides, very generous with his money, which the young couple needed frequently. Yanovitsky's chances of getting work appeared at first to be very slim, both in St. Petersburg and in Moscow. Though he was able to get an odd job from time to time, he was forced to depend mostly on his friends and on Vassily Kokaoulin.

A true Kokaoulin, Lyubochka longed to have children, but her husband's uncertain situation made him reluctant to have a family. She suffered a great deal because of this. The Kokaoulin family were inclined to consider it selfishness on the part of Yanovitsky, but Lyubochka's love for him silenced all protest. She bore her unhappiness quietly, sharing it only with her father.

But Vassily's nerves were tired. He did not want to go back to living alone in Alushta. In spite of his long years of retirement, he had always kept in occasional touch with the gold-mine affairs in Bodaybo. Old friends from Bodaybo once in a while came to see him,

Sonya, mother of the composer, about 1911.

Lyubochka and her father about 1910.

and he had been approached, though not officially, while he was living in the Crimea with his wife, and offered a position at the mines at double his previous salary. But he always declined. Now again in 1908, perhaps owing to the tragedies of the last few years, his interests turned toward Bodaybo. In a scientific and technical magazine, *Gold and Platinum*, in the issue of January 15, 1909, appears a long and very detailed article written by Vassily Kokaoulin, under the title: "Notes on the Gold Industry in the Regions of Olekma and Vitim." The article was a detailed summary of all the improvements that Kokaoulin had tried to bring about during his last years at Bodaybo. Apparently, after ten years had gone by, the daily needs of the miners and of the industry remained the same.

It was decided in 1910 to sell the Lena Gold Mines. Vassily Kokaoulin was asked officially to come to Bodaybo and take charge of the final arrangements. He decided to accept. As he said to Sonya: "The offer is very inviting, and old friends and old surroundings draw me there."

Sonya accompanied her father to the station and sat with him in a second-class car, where he always preferred to travel. The train was very late in leaving. Sonya had sat with her father for several hours, and the warning bell had still not rung for the departure. Finally he told her not to wait but to go home to her children. As she left, Sonya noticed that her father, who was only fifty-nine, looked seventy. She realized for the first time how the years had broken this calm and patient man.

Vassily Kokaoulin spent that winter of 1910 living alone in Bodaybo with his servant, in his old home, where once the cries and laughter of his children had filled the rooms. In the many letters that he wrote to his family he described the warm welcome he had received from old friends, and the changes he had found. The workmen, he wrote, were still not provided with proper housing, and their cooking was still done over great outdoor fires. The senseless cutting down of trees to provide fuel for these continuous fires had resulted as Kokaoulin had predicted — much of the great taiga that he had seen when he arrived years ago was gone, leaving acres of bare ground, dotted with stumps and looking like a desert. The old barn that Alexandra had used for the orchestra had partly burned and then collapsed; but the garden that she had planted with such care, in soil that had not known even grass, was still flourishing and had blossomed and spread.

Late on the evening of the 23rd of February 1911, the night of Sonya's birthday, Vassily Kokaoulin sat at his desk and wrote a letter to his oldest daughter, Vera. He said that he had just finished his work, he had accomplished everything he had planned, and his mission in Bodaybo was fulfilled. He would only wait for the opening of the roads and would return to St. Petersburg to be with his children. He wrote that he was tired but content and that he would write to all of them in detail tomorrow.

On the next morning, when his valet came as usual to call him for breakfast, Vassily Kokaoulin was deep in a sleep from which he would never awaken. He was buried with honor in the courtyard of the little church at the end of the barren square that his children had seen so often through the windows of the nursery.

A year and a half later, thousands of miners streamed silently out of Bodaybo after the Lena slaughter, never to return; and as they passed the grave of Vassily Kokaoulin, of their "Father Kokaoulin" whom they remembered, they took off their caps and made the sign of the cross.

* * *

Sonya and Dmitri were at this time in their early thirties. Dmitri's hair was thinning and he now had to wear a pince-nez but he was still the same cheerful, happy-go-lucky fellow that his friends had all known in his student days. He still sang all the new "romances" to Sonya's accompaniment, played duets with her on the piano, and carried a pile of music with him whenever they went to see friends, for he was always asked to sing.

He kept his work completely apart from his family and never discussed it at home. He gave all his money to Sonya and kept for himself only enough "to buy tobacco for his pipe." Their financial situation had improved steadily, for Dmitri was now the general manager of Irinovka, the Rennenkampf estate. He and his wife went to concerts and had subscription tickets to the Mariinsky Theater. They also entertained a great deal. Sonya gradually weeded out most of the Siberian friends of Dmitri's student days because, for her, there was too much of the "moujik" about them and in these days she sought a different society. Dmitri took all this reform very good-naturedly and only retained, in spite of all that Sonya could do, his heavy gait and his rough, Siberian-peasant way of speaking. Sonya would have despaired of his slangy speech except that she knew his gay and lovable disposition always won him friends wherever he went. "Sonya, Sonya," he would say, shaking his head and looking at her over the top of his glasses, "I'm a bad one. Squirt me another glass of tea."

He never seemed to take anything seriously; he was never worried and always full of fun. He had a passion for gadgets — new cigarette-lighters, tiny knives, fancy boxes for all purposes, and any wire or ring puzzles he could find; these he worked over for hours, with his children sitting on the floor around him. He loved mystery stories and collected a whole library of them from second-hand book shops. But, above all, he liked games of solitaire. Whenever he came home with a new version he would say: "Now, this is the solitaire Napoleon played," and the whole family sat and watched him work out the game.

In the summer the children ran barefoot about

Irinovka, gathering mushrooms and berries; in the winter they played in a little garden across from their house on Nikolaevskaya Street. They were brought up in much the same way as Sonya had been in Bodaybo in that they never had many playthings and had to invent their own games from what they found around them. This, Sonya felt, would develop their imagination. They had a great sense of fun, and Sonya always remembered with amusement the day a friend of hers came to see her; the two youngsters, Mitya and Zoya, ran out to greet the stranger and, as though they had rehearsed all this before, flopped simultaneously to their knees and began bowing low, touching their foreheads to the floor. They kept up this performance until they were convulsed with laughter and had to run from the room. A moment later they returned hand in hand, completely serious, and sang for the guest an old Russian song which they had heard their mother sing.

Marusia, who was eight, was already going to school and had begun her piano study with her mother. Sonya was an excellent teacher, and she occasionally gave lessons free of charge to her friends. Zoya and Mitya were joined in their studies by their playmates, the Rennenkampf children. They were taught by a German governess and Sonya approved of this early opportunity of their learning a foreign language, although she could not resist making fun of the "fräulein" in her old mocking manner.

Adolf Rennenkampf engaged a dancing-master for

them — Yakovlev of the Mariinsky Theater, under whose tutelage had passed some of the best ballerinas in the Russian ballet. It was from this man that little Mitya and his sisters learned their first pirouettes and entrechats. Mitya was slightly scornful of these ballet steps and had more fun in the hopak, a real man's dance. Hands on hips and heels flying, he would "tear off" a hopak like a little whirlwind. Marusia, a husky little girl with light hair and lively black eyes, was the most talented of them all, and Yakovlev urged Sonya to let her daughter become a ballerina.

When Nadejda came to visit them they would gather around her for stories of that far-off mysterious land, Siberia, where their father and mother had come from. She regaled them with tales of racing troikas and of packs of wolves, of the bear mother who had been her first nurse; she told them how bitter cold it was and how they used to throw snow mixed with water against the sides of the house so that it would freeze into ice and keep them warm inside. She told them of the night the valet Dmitri had come to tell them about a party their parents were attending. "It is all lit up with Chinese lanterns," he had told them, "and they have brought dancing bears and a whole band to play for them." He paused there before adding his finishing touch: "And on tight-ropes over the people's heads cats walk back and forth, with red flames spitting from their green eyes!" "Your mother wanted to see the cats," Nadejda told Mitya and Zoya, "and so we got

58

out of bed in the middle of the night and got dressed and went to see. And sure enough, there they were!" Mitya, whose eyes were popping, said solemnly that he had seen lots of cats in St. Petersburg, but there was no flame spitting from their eyes. "Ah," said Nadejda, "but these were Siberian cats!"

In the winter of 1911 Sonya and Nadejda took the children for the first time to the opera — to see Rimsky-Korsakov's *Czar Saltan's Fairy Tale*. The excitement that reigned in the house while their mother was dressing them for their first theater party could be compared only to Sonya's and Nadejda's when they were being taken to see the flame-spitting cats in Bodaybo. For now the children would see a story as enthralling as one of Nadejda's come to life before their very eyes.

They sat breathless through the performance, and the next day little Mitya surprised the family with his unusual memory and ear. He recited and sang correctly most of the opera. Sonya did not conclude from this, however, that her son was a musical genius or a child prodigy; she kept to her decision that he would take up his music in due time, as Marusia had done, and that meanwhile he would play and grow up as any child does.

* * *

Lyubochka's health was growing steadily worse. She had a constant fever of 101° and 102° and the shock of her father's death aggravated a case of tuberculosis that already needed serious attention. Her life with Yano-vitsky was a mixture of happiness and sorrow and was made still more uneven by the fact that her illness forced her to make trips to different sanatoriums in Germany every year. These sporadic journeys did more damage to her health than good, for she was torn with loneliness for her husband and her country. When the first World War broke out, Lyubochka was in Reichen-hall, her health dangerously worse. Nadejda came from Göttingen, where she was taking her degree, and joined her sister. The last the Shostakovich family heard of them, they were in Munich trying to arrange with the German authorities to go to Switzerland.

In 1915 Nadejda returned to Nikolaevskaya Street and brought with her the tragic story of Lyubochka's death. The children remembered their young aunt well, for they had been very fond of her and she had spent all of her time with them whenever she was in St. Peters-burg. She and little Mitya had been fast friends, and this was the first deep grief to come into the boy's life. The family listened in tears as Nadejda told her story.

She had taken Lyubochka to a sanatorium in Leysin, Switzerland, near Montreux, where they arrived in October 1914. The doctor told Nadejda that he did not expect Lyubochka to last until Christmas, and from then on Nadejda never left her sister alone and slept on a couch in her room at night. Lyubochka was now unable to leave her bed, and through the large window in her room she and Nadejda would watch the sun go down beyond the snow-covered peak of the Dent-du-Midi; they could look far down into the Rhone Valley and on moonlight nights they were held spellbound by the beauty of the broken clouds that hung above it.

Lyubochka was wasting away from day to day and it was no longer necessary for the doctor to tell Nadejda how critical her condition was. She was nervous and restless. Now that they were in a neutral country they received many letters from home, from Lyubochka's student friends, painters, and writers. But there was no letter from Yanovitsky. Lyubochka wrote often to him, and finally even Nadejda wrote, asking him to answer. They had heard through Sonya and other friends that he was well and that their letters reached him. But there was no word from him.

On December 2 Lyubochka was feeling well and in high spirits. She asked her sister to entertain her, and Nadejda picked up *War and Peace*. "I started to read to her, and suddenly her head fell forward on her chest. I ran for the doctor. When he returned from Lyubochka's room into the corridor, he put his hand on my shoulder and said, simply: '*C'est la fin.*' I walked back quietly to my sister. She was lying on her side, holding her wrist with her other hand. She looked at me and I guess she read in my face that I knew she was dying. Our eyes met and her last words were in Russian: 'There is no more pulse.' The nurse took her hand and said that her pulse was all right. Lyubochka looked at the nurse and smiled at me, but she had no strength for another word. Her breathing became slower and slower and finally stopped. A thin line of perspiration appeared on her forehead."

Nadejda sat for a long time beside her sister. Gradually the lines of sickness and sorrow disappeared from Lyubochka's face, and a quiet peace settled over it. Nadejda remembered what her father had told her in Alushta — how, in the hour after her mother had died, the years fell away from her and she looked once more as she had on the day he married her.

Nadejda covered her sister's body in the coffin with white cyclamen, the same flowers that Lyubochka had held in her hands when she married Yanovitsky in the Kresti prison.

She was buried three days later in the little hillside cemetery of the sanatorium, with only Nadejda and a priest in attendance.

*   *   *

The Shostakovich family had moved to a new apartment on Nikolaevskaya Street; it was on the opposite side of the street, on the fifth floor of Number 9. After the declaration of war Dmitri had taken a position as commercial manager of Promet, a war industry making shells and ammunition. Besides the higher salary, the family had two cars at their disposal, one for Dmitri's business and one for the family's personal use.

Nadejda found them at a high pitch of patriotic fervor which had swept the whole country. She came

under a great deal of criticism because she remembered
with affection her good friends in Göttingen and was
not yet ready for any wholesale condemnation of the
German race. But here Sonya showed one of her stubbornly unreasonable traits: when she took to heart
what she believed to be a great cause, she would see
nothing but her own side. She who loved her sister and
would do anything for her was ready to condemn her
as a traitor merely for having gone to study in Germany. She called Nadejda a German for not leaving
the enemy country sooner. Nadejda explained almost
in tears that Lyubochka had been her sole reason for
staying; but the more she protested, the more unreasonable Sonya became, and it was always Dmitri who
had to make peace between them. "Now," he would
say to Sonya, "leave Nadejda alone and stop nagging
at her; she is not that bad."

The children were always delighted to hear stories
about Germany because Nadejda made them entertaining. Mitya liked the one about how Nadejda used
to go every day to the local post office in Reichenhall
for the mail; here she watched the little blackboard
that announced the interruption in postal communications. It read at first that postal communications had
been suspended *"mit Serbien und Russland"*; then
later: *"mit Serbien, Russland, Frankreich und Belgien"*; and finally: *"mit Serbien, Russland, Frankreich,
Belgien und England."* Nadejda told Mitya, much to
his merriment, how economical the Germans were —

they never rewrote the message on the blackboard, they merely added a comma and moved the *"und."* These stories she told every Saturday, when the children held their own "little tea" in the nursery, at which small Zoya was the hostess; the table, the samovar, and the cups were all scaled down to the children's size.

Marusia had worked diligently at her studies and at the piano and she surprised Nadejda by the rapidity of her small fingers on the keyboard. Mitya, with his light hair and gray eyes, was a dreamy child and lay often on his back staring into space. He was at this time much interested in astronomy and followed Nadejda around asking her interminable questions about the stars. He was also reading all the stories of adventure and exploration he could find and his temporary hero was Fridtjof Nansen.

The summer of 1916, when the family went back to Irinovka, Mitya had his first lessons on the piano with his mother. She was surprised how easily he learned and memorized his little pieces. Nadejda remembers very well the first time Mitya improvised for her. He sat down at the piano one evening and, with an absorbed expression on his handsome little face, started to make up a story.

"Here is a snow-covered village far away —" a run and the beginning of a little tune accompanied his words — "moonlight is shining on the empty road — here is a little house lit by a candle —" Mitya played his tune and then, looking slyly at his aunt over the top

Sonya Shostakovich and her children, Mitya, Zoya, and Marusia; taken at Irinovka in 1911.

of the piano, he suddenly flicked a note high in the treble — "Somebody peeks in the window."

But these improvisations were rare; music was not yet all-absorbing, and the children spent most of the time with their playmates. Mitya grew very fond of Jurgensen, who was the handy man around the estate. Whenever things didn't go as Mitya liked them at home, he would declare, pouting: "Well then, I'll go and live with Jurgensen." One day, when he had misbehaved and Sonya had scolded him, he again threatened to leave. "All right," said Sonya, "get dressed. I'll take you myself to Jurgensen." Muttering to himself, Mitya dressed very quickly and Sonya took him firmly by the hand and they started out across the field for Jurgensen's house. At first Mitya swaggered along bravely. Then gradually Sonya felt his pace slacken and lag; then his hand began slowly to slip out of hers, finger by finger. Suddenly he burst into tears, turned, and ran back home as fast as he could.

In the fall Sonya returned early to Petrograd because the children had to start school. Marusia was a pupil in one of the best schools in Petrograd, that of Mme Stayunin; Mitya entered the private school of Shidlovsky. This was one of many progressive schools that had sprung up throughout Russia after the first revolution of 1905, in an effort to get away from the regimentation of the government high schools. The children of the Russian intelligentsia and of parents of liberal ideas were sent to these new schools.

From the progress that Mitya was making in his piano lessons with his mother, Sonya decided that her son's talent needed professional guidance and she took him, along with Marusia, to the Glyasser music school. Glyasser was a typical Petrograd German with an "artistic" appearance, a tall man with a thick mane of gray hair.

It was not long before Glyasser recognized in Sonya a competent musician with taste and a sound sense of criticism far above the average musical amateur. She was asked to the school often as adviser and as judge for examinations. During Mitya's first year there, he composed his first piece, *Theme and Variations*; this little composition was never written down, but Mitya played it often for his family, and in later years used it as an encore in his concerts.

The Shostakovich family was not very deeply affected by the war, for, in spite of the bad news from the front and the rising price of living, the capital was full of gaiety and careless optimism. It was only through the letters from Nadejda in the winter of 1915–16 that the family got a glimpse of what actually was going on throughout Russia in the second year of the war.

Nadejda had left early in the fall of 1915 to take a position in Ekaterinburg. She was to work as a physicist in one of the observatories, which were all under the direction of Prince Galitzin. That Christmas she spent with Vera, her oldest sister, whom she had not seen in nine years. In Omsk, where Vera was living with her family, Nadejda found again the atmosphere that she had almost forgotten — that of political and revolutionary excitement. This provincial town in Siberia was thousands of miles away from the government and therefore enjoyed more freedom of speech and openness of intercourse among the liberals than did the capital. Vera's house was the center of debates between the older moderate liberals and the hot-headed youth. Nadejda received a clearer and more accurate picture of the national state of affairs here than the Shostakoviches could possibly have on Nikolaevskaya Street. She heard of the constant shifting of ministers — nicknamed "the ministers' leap-frog" — of the cases of treason, the corruption existing in the war industries; and she heard also for the first time of the Siberian peasant whose evil influence ruled the house of Romanov.

The air "smelt of storm."

Chapter
5.

ON the morning of the 27th of February 1917
Sonya and Nadejda had a late breakfast by themselves,
since they had been out to the theater the night before.
The children had already gone to school and Dmitri
was away at work. The janitor who brought up their
mail was full of news. He told them that strange things
were going on in the city; the Nevsky was packed with
crowds of people, streaming into it from all sides; the
police, the army, and the Cossacks were riding up and
down keeping order, but neither the Cossacks nor the
soldiers were molesting or trying to disperse the crowd.
The janitor said that he himself had seen the Cossacks
leaning down from their horses, joking and talking with
the people.

Sasha, the cook, came later with the same report.
She said that everyone in the neighborhood was excited
and that many had come out into the street. The rumor
was that the police captain had demanded that the
Cossacks shoot into the crowd, but that the Cossack

officer had slashed the extended arm off of the captain as he was giving that order.

"This looks like revolution," said Sonya, and she went down to the street to look herself. She, too, saw the mob that was moving slowly up the Nevsky, with the army and the Cossacks riding with them. She saw the helpless police standing idly by, and she heard those around her saying that the people had stood all night in queues for bread, and when in the morning the bread had been refused, they had started to demonstrate.

As she went back into her house, she passed the doorman. He said to her: "Well, ma'am, what is it? A revolution, isn't it?" The servants ran in and out, relaying bits of news, their eyes shining with excitement; people on the streets greeted one another with a smile, and the general air was more of holiday than of upheaval.

Sonya called Dmitri at his office and he told her to have the children brought home from school. He told her that the Kresti prison had been broken open, and that the headquarters of the Okhranka had been set afire. He still had an errand to do, but he assured Sonya that he would be home soon. Sonya immediately sent Sasha to get Mitya, and some friends brought Zoya and Marusia home. Mitya burst into the apartment full of excitement and bravado, declaring that there was nothing to be afraid of and that Sasha's stories of a revolution were only women's chatter. However,

Sasha's account of Mitya's bravery was a little different. All the way home through the excited crowds he had kept repeating: "There's no revolution, it's all nonsense"; but he clung tightly to her skirts just the same.

The superintendent was walking up and down in front of the house with a large red bow in his lapel. According to the cook, the story was that when the Kresti was opened, one of the prisoners, a young student, had appeared in the back yard looking for the superintendent, who, it seemed, had denounced him and therefore had been responsible for his going to prison. At the sight of the young avenger and his friends, the unfortunate superintendent had fallen to his knees and implored forgiveness. This having been granted, the restored and chastened man had decorated himself with the most conspicuous red bow he could find and was now parading it in front of the house and beaming defiance of the Imperial government.

Little Mitya begged Sonya to fix bows for them as big as the superintendent's and to let them go out on the street with the rest of the people. Sonya pinned a few red ribbons on them and sent them downstairs, telling them to stay in front of the house. The telephone was ringing constantly; friends called to relate the latest news and to find out what Sonya knew. Nadejda went into the kitchen and tried to explain the meaning of revolution to the servants — but most unsuccessfully.

During the next few days, although life went on

much as usual, with the shops open and the people going to work, the actual facts behind the trouble began to sift through. The murder of Rasputin, the complete sway the Czarina held over her weakling husband, the preparations for the coup that was to overthrow the Czar, his abdication, and the formation of a temporary government — all this that had been under a thick blanket of censorship now was beginning to be known.

The power of the Romanovs, who had held Russia in their grip for three hundred years, was suddenly no more. The fight for freedom, for which every muscle of the revolutionary element had been strained for so long — this fight seemed all at once to have been won, perhaps with that one stroke of the Cossack's saber that had taken off the policeman's arm. "We will no longer shoot into our own people." The banners of freedom waved over all Russia.

Rumors that the Czar's abdication was just another scheming trick to put him, eventually, back in absolute power — that he had left his headquarters at the front only to join his wife and children — that his train had been met and shunted off in a different direction by the soldiers, who were now loyal to the people — these items of news were of secondary importance. For the freedom that had brought fathers, husbands, and sons out of the Kresti and back from Siberia filled the air, and old and young alike were carried away by Russia's "resurrection."

This festive spirit spread even to the children; Mitya

was infected with it and composed a short piece which he called *Hymn to Liberty*.

But the precarious balance of a "bloodless Revolution" could not be kept for long. The victims of violence on both sides grew steadily in number, and soon funerals for those who had died for the Revolution in its first days were being held throughout Russia. A gigantic funeral procession filled the streets and avenues of Petrograd on the way to the Marsovo Field, where the bodies were to be put into one common grave. A great sea of people moved solemnly up the Nevsky Prospekt — soldiers, sailors, workmen, students, and the new "free citizens" of the capital; on their shoulders rocked the coffins covered with brilliant red banners. The procession moved slowly between the packed lines of spectators, to the strains of the revolutionary funeral song: *You Fell Victims in the Fatal Struggle*. Platforms had been erected on the street corners, and here the procession stopped while men made speeches in the name of freedom, revolution, and the dead. Clinging to trees and lamp-posts, leaning from windows and balconies, perched on roofs and on fences, men and women watched the impressive parade; they lifted their children to their shoulders so that they, too, might see. They had been gathering since early morning, and many of them had stood shivering in the cold dawn wind of that gray March day, awaiting the procession.

The Shostakovich family was there in the crowd and

the children had climbed to the top of an iron fence surrounding an old churchyard. The sad air of the funeral song filled their hearts with a strange pain and pride.

When the tired family returned home that evening, Mitya went to the piano and played quietly for a long time; he might have been thinking of a tragic incident that he had witnessed a few days before and which had left a deep impression on him — the brutal killing of a small boy by a policeman.[1] Then he played to them the piece he had just composed, his *Funeral March for the Victims of the Revolution*. This and his *Hymn to Liberty* were the two things he was always asked to play when anyone came to the house.[2]

Though the excitement of these days in Petrograd had penetrated every home, the life of its citizens went on without interruption. The Shostakovich children continued their schooling and Mitya took his lessons at Glyasser's music school as usual. In the spring of 1917 he made his first public appearance at the piano. At the regular school recital, attended by the mothers and other relatives of the pupils, the children performed the pieces they had learned. Mitya, dressed in long trousers and a sailor jacket, came quietly onto the platform and took his place at the instrument. He looked thoughtfully at his audience and then played the open-

[1] In Shostakovich's Second Symphony, dedicated to the October Revolution, and published in 1927, this incident was put into music in an episode before the entrance of the chorus.

[2] These two pieces were never written down.

ing chords of his piece — Handel's Largo. As the first notes of the melody sang out, the audience leaned forward with sudden interest. Many children at that recital played just as correctly as did Mitya, but in this simple piece the hearers sensed that there was something more to the performance than the correct playing of the notes.

There is a story that Tolstoy tells about the painter Bryulov. "In correcting a pupil's study, Bryulov just touched it up in a few places and the poor, dead study suddenly revived. 'You have touched it up just a little bit and all is changed,' said one of the pupils. 'Art begins where the *"little bit"* begins,' said Bryulov." Tolstoy concludes by saying: "The remark is true of all the arts, but its justice is particularly noticeable in the performance of music."

Evidently Mitya had that "little bit."

Even Sonya and Nadejda were surprised at the deep impression Mitya had created with the easy piece that they had heard him practice day after day.

Marusia played at this recital too, a far more advanced piece than Mitya's. She played it well, but, as Sonya said, she lacked the love of playing that a performer should have. Marusia herself, who adored her brother, was far more excited about his performance than her own.

When Dmitri came home that evening, he was told by the elated family of the success of his son and was filled with pride. Mitya, who could not understand the fuss they were making over him, had gone into the courtyard to play with his friends and had forgotten all about it.

His family began to discuss his future seriously. Those who had heard the recital had congratulated Sonya, predicting great things for her son and calling him a "*Wunderkind.*" Sonya wondered whether she should enter him immediately in the Petrograd Conservatory, but, taking into account his youth and the uncertainty of the times, they decided to wait awhile.

*   *   *

The three phases of the 1917 Revolution — the overthrow of czarism and the establishment of the provisional government, the unsuccessful armed uprising of the Bolsheviks in July, and finally the October Revolution — all took place in the capital under the eyes of its citizens. The streets of Petrograd were filled with restless civilians, soldiers, and sailors, gathering for meetings, arguing on street corners. Banners were hung on lamp-posts, pamphlets were strewn about the sidewalks, posters and placards were pasted on the walls. The pushing throng moved slowly and aimlessly as though at a fair; soldiers carrying their heavy rifles, many of them deserters from the collapsing front, stood on street corners and sold "souvenirs" that they had stolen or looted — costly vases, musical instruments, officers' leather boots. Sailors stood about in groups, with strings of cartridges around their necks and huge revolvers swinging from their belts; men in brilliant uniforms, who had heretofore only been seen in parades of their regiments, now prowled the streets alone like stray cats; Cossacks, with their tall fur hats on the back of their heads, took rides on the street-cars. To the din of the crowded streets were added the cries of small boys selling newspapers as they dodged about the feet of the moving throng. In addition to the regular papers, new ones were constantly appearing, which sprang into print for a few days and then dropped as suddenly out of circulation; every paper put out many extras during the course of a day and besides these were the news bulletins, issued by different parties and printed on brightly colored paper, which were bought up by the news-hungry crowd as soon as they appeared. Each new bulletin started endless debates on the future of Russia and the newly gained liberty.

The Shostakovich children continued to go to school and work at their music, but the excitement of these times was like a continual parade to them, and what their alert young minds absorbed of its significance had much to do with the development of their maturity. Incidents often happened to them that required explanations and gradually they came to know that the Revolution was affecting everybody. Once when they were coming home from school in the car that they had been using for several years, they were stopped by two armed soldiers, who jumped onto the running board and told Sonya that the car was being "requisitioned."

Sonya asked them if they would let her go first to the house. Her driver began to get angry at the soldiers, but Sonya calmed him, and after they were driven home, she turned the car over to them.

That summer Sonya took the children back to Irinovka, but Dmitri and Nadejda remained in the city and were witnesses of the July uprising of the Bolsheviks. From July 16 to the 18th the streets of Petrograd were turned into a battlefield. Both Dmitri and Nadejda — drawn, as human beings so strangely are, to danger — exposed themselves often to stray bullets when their curiosity took them onto the streets.

Whenever they went to Irinovka the children were eager to hear all the details of the events their parents were discussing. They wanted to know about the Revolution and its meaning — about Lenin, about Plekhanov and Karl Marx. Neither Dmitri nor Sonya felt they could convey the facts simply enough for the children's minds and Nadejda undertook to tell them all she knew about it; she was, in a way, the authority, for she alone of the three adults had at one time been a member of a revolutionary party. The 1905 revolution was naturally not in Mitya's history books, but his teachers had said that in order to understand the events of 1917 one should have a clear picture of those of 1905, and he plagued Nadejda to tell him about it. All she could tell a boy of eleven was the story of the Moscow uprising that she had witnessed herself. The last flash of the revolution of 1905, its tragic finale, was that uprising in Moscow in December. For thirteen days the Moscow revolutionists fought the cavalry and artillery of the government. They erected clumsy barricades and defended themselves with revolvers against the machine guns that had been hoisted on the belfries of the cathedrals.

"As soon as I heard of the uprising," said Nadejda, "I took a cab to the clinic where my husband, Dr. Galli, was on duty. I told him that it was necessary to arrange a first-aid station at once. I collected the necessary dressings and with the help of some students I took them to the Stroganovskaya School, where the wounded were already being brought in. We cared for all, whether revolutionists or soldiers. Although someone reported us and we had to flee the next day, we managed to take all the wounded to a hospital. We had to walk home across what seemed to us like the whole of Moscow. It was pitch dark; the sky was red from the burning buildings and from the huge bonfires which the soldiers had built to keep themselves warm.

"The next day the barricades and the fighting reached our quarters. It wasn't safe to cross the streets at any time, as the soldiers and Cossacks were sniping from the windows and almost killed my husband and me as we were on our way to see his sister, who was ill. The police were searching from house to house for students and revolutionists, and the panicky workers needed organization. They asked me, as a member of the party, to lend my apartment for one of their meetings. My room was one cloud of cigarette smoke when suddenly my husband came to tell us that the police were coming to search. We threw the windows wide open to air the place, and while my guests left, one by one, I hid all traces of the meeting."

Nadejda told Mitya of the unnecessary cruelty with which the Moscow uprising was crushed. Prisoners were executed without trial; houses and factories were bombarded and destroyed; the terrorized population was treated like a conquered enemy. Not satisfied with its military triumphs, the government sent its soldiers on a punitive expedition into the Moscow region. The orders from the high authorities: "Take no prisoners; act without mercy," were carried out to the letter.

These revolutionary stories, together with the often told account of his uncle's trial, were strong fare for the imaginative mind of the eleven-year-old boy, and Mitya would find powerful expression for them in later years.

*   *   *

In the October days of the final struggle the Bolsheviks found support even among the soldiers on whom the provisional government relied. There were constant demonstrations and fighting in the streets, and the cruiser *Aurora*, which had been sent up the Neva in July, opened fire and shelled the Winter Palace. The citizens of Petrograd, who had once celebrated their "bloodless revolution" with a great parade and later mourned its first victims, now grimly joined the soldiers

79

and sailors in the bitterest fighting their city had ever known. Even the children, carrying their copy-books to school, were drawn into the storm. On the way to and from school they had to push through crowds of fiercely debating soldiers and civilians. Later in life Mitya stated proudly: "I met the October Revolution on the street." The schools tried to keep up a regular routine, but the events outside on the streets were often far more absorbing to the students than the lectures in the classrooms. In the same school with Mitya were the children of Kerensky and also of Trotsky; the children took sides and were even more violent in their reactions than their parents.

In 1918, on the 3rd of March, the Russians finally signed the peace treaty of Brest-Litovsk. The terms dictated by the Germans were disastrous for Russia, but the Bolshevik government, which had started negotiations as soon as it had come into power, was no longer in a position to bargain, for the country was in chaos. Under this treaty the Ukraine, Poland, Finland, Lithuania, Estonia, and Latvia received their independence. Part of Transcaucasia was ceded to Turkey and the rest of it formed independent republics. Russia lost 25 per cent of her total population, 27 per cent of her arable land, 32 per cent of her average crops, 26 per cent of her railway system, 33 per cent of her manufacturing industries, 73 per cent of her iron industry, and 75 per cent of her coal fields. Besides the casualties of 2,500,-000 dead and mutilated, she had to pay a large war indemnity. Added to this, the country's resources had been further sapped by civil war, and inflation was in full swing. The economic situation in Petrograd was at its worst. The government had nationalized private property; the peasants refused to supply the cities with food since the cities had nothing to offer in exchange; and the value of money was dropping rapidly. Famine was imminent.

The Shostakovich family had had no servants since the beginning of the revolution and either Sonya made up their meals from what they received with their ration cards or they brought their food home from one of the government eating-houses. Sonya had to improvise from the meager supplies they were able to get by standing in long-queues. She even managed to arrange little parties for her children on their birthdays. But most of the time there was scarcely enough to keep alive on. Mitya, although he was a frail child, did not seem to mind these privations, however. When he came home from school he would toss aside his books and look through the cupboards for a bit to eat; if, as often happened, there was nothing to be had, he would go without complaint down to the courtyard to play.

Their situation was somewhat relieved by the sale of the Kokaoulin estate in Alushta; this was managed by Nadejda in Ekaterinburg, where she was a professor at the university. With the money, Nadejda purchased precious stones such as diamonds and emeralds; these were a good investment since money was losing value daily. She sent the stones by friends to the Shostakovich family in Petrograd so that they in turn could exchange them for the supplies they needed.

The relief was only temporary, however, and when Nadejda arrived in Petrograd in the summer of 1919 the Shostakovich children greeted her with cries of "We are hungry, Aunt Nadia, we are hungry!" Nadejda had brought with her bags of buckwheat groats, from which is made the Russian porridge called *kasha*; this was a rare delicacy in Ekaterinburg, but the children's faces dropped when they saw it, and they said sadly: "That's all we've been living on!"

By this time money had completely lost its value; all purchases were made by exchange. One heard on the streets: "We are living now on our grand piano," and "*We* are living on the bedroom curtains and father's old watch!" Zoya and her aunt Nadia went one day to the Petrograd Zoo and witnessed the sad spectacle of the gaunt and hungry elephants snatching hats from people's heads and swallowing them. The one topic of burning interest was food; there were interminable discussions about what could be obtained with the ration cards and what might be expected in the future, and what was to be had from the government eating-houses, where the food was hardly fit for animals. One night Marusia brought back from one of these eating-houses a pailful of soup to eke out the evening meal. She seemed rather subdued as she watched the family swallowing it with gusto and finally she could bear it no longer. She confessed that the attendant at the eating-house had told everyone, as he dished out the soup, that a rat had been found at the bottom of the tureen. He added that the soup was all there was to be had, however, and that if anyone objected he would have to do without anything.

Dried codfish and cans of sardines were the main articles that the government handed out to the people; upon receiving them, everyone would immediately try to exchange them for something else, only to be greeted with the words: "We don't want any more sardines *or* codfish!"

No rents were paid, there were no longer any janitors for the apartment houses, and the tenants formed "house committees" to take care of the janitors' duties co-operatively. Even the pay of the professors was very irregular, though professors were considered to be in a privileged class. Once they were not paid for four summer months; when they applied for this back pay, the reply was: "Here is money for one month; you lived through the other three, so why do you need the money for them now?"

In those days Dmitri held a position with Vnezh-Torg, a new government office organized to handle trade outside of Russia. The family no longer went to Irinovka, but remained in their apartment on Niko-laevskaya Street. Dmitri, with his usual energy, spent all of his free time getting the necessary supplies of food for his family. On the estate of Irinovka there was still one cow left, Kyra by name, and Dmitri used to go there to get the supply of milk. He never complained and never lost his good humor; his friends always remarked that he could finish a meal of sausage and soggy bread, fill his pipe with dusty tobacco shavings, and lean back and light up as though he had just finished a banquet and were smoking a Havana cigar with his coffee.

Mitya and Marusia were now studying in the Petrograd Conservatory of Music. Sonya had decided that though both children were making progress at Glyasser's school, it was time now for them to enter the conservatory. To the great sadness of old Glyasser, she took them to study with Rosanova. Professor Rosanova had been Sonya's own teacher during the years Sonya had gone to the conservatory. During his first year there Mitya composed a Scherzo and eight Preludes for the piano, which remain in manuscript form. Glazunov, then the director of the conservatory, heard the compositions of the thirteen-year-old boy and advised him to join the class in composition under Professor Maximilian Steinberg.

*   *   *

In the second week of February 1922 Mitya's father suddenly fell ill. He came home one day complaining of a headache; he was quiet and subdued and went to bed without his usual joking. At first Sonya thought he might have caught a cold out in the raw weather, during one of his distant errands to the outskirts of the city looking for supplies, or during one of the nights when it was his turn among the members of the "house committee" to discharge the duties of janitor.

Sonya kept him in bed; he had no fever, but felt very tired and weak. Three days passed and he was getting no better; he still complained of headache and continued to grow weaker. Sonya called in a doctor from the neighborhood, a woman, since their own doctor was away. This woman doctor also thought at first that Dmitri had a cold. Pneumonia was at that time raging through the city; but the fact that he had no fever puzzled her. His pulse had gone up to 120 and the doctor thought that digitalis should be given to strengthen his heart and stabilize his pulse.

But medical supplies in the city were even harder to get than food, and it proved impossible to secure any digitalis. It can now be recognized by the symptoms that Dmitri was the victim of a heart ailment that resulted in a blood-clot on his brain. He himself may never have realized that anything was wrong with his heart, but undoubtedly the physical and mental strain that he had been subjected to for the last several years had taken effect. For a week longer he lay in bed sinking slowly, and then, on the 24th of February, he quietly died in full consciousness.

The family was plunged into indescribable grief. There were no immediate relatives at the time in Petrograd; Jasha was far away in Rostov and couldn't leave his work. The children sent a telegram to Nadejda in Ekaterinburg: "Father died. Come immediately."

It was two weeks before Nadejda could get to Petrograd, and when she arrived she found the family in deep mourning. There was a hollow feeling in the pit of her stomach when she saw how lifeless the house was without Dmitri's warm gaiety.

The death of Dmitri was not only an emotional but also a financial blow; besides being the gay spirit that had pulled the family through all their difficulties, he had been their sole means of support. Sonya had lost her adored husband, and, in her early forties, found herself at the head of a family which, though musically and artistically endowed, was far from being ready for self-support. Mitya was sixteen, Marusia nineteen, and Zoya fourteen, and their school days were not yet over.

Twenty years before, Sonya would have had no trouble finding a position as a teacher because of her brilliant education; but now, with no experience and in the changed conditions of living, she had no chance in competition with the young who were looking for work. Her musical education, never completed, would not have opened her a position at any school, and as for private pupils, one could hardly depend on them in those days.

It was fortunate that while Dmitri was still alive, she had taken, out of curiosity, a course in stenography and typing; this proved now to be the sole means of the family's livelihood. Through old friends, Sonya was given a position as typist in the Chamber of Weights and Measures, where all the Kokaoulins were so well liked.

Nadejda and her second husband, Professor Shohat, whom she had married after the death of Dr. Galli, moved into the Shostakovich apartment to keep the bereaved family company and to share with them whatever they received on their ration cards. They, being professors, received extra supplies, which came under the heading of "Academic Rations."

*   *   *

Sonya had a deep faith in her son's talent, and she decided that he should leave school so that he could devote more time to his music, which was to be his profession.

For the last three years Mitya had been studying at the Stayunin School, but his complete inability to concentrate on mathematical problems was a constant trouble to him and to his teachers. One of his teachers relates how, looking earnestly through his horn-rimmed glasses and rumpling his light hair, he would say: "Well, what is going to happen to me? . . . I just can't concentrate on figures, my head is full of sounds."

After his teachers had consulted with Sonya, it was decided that Mitya should complete the rest of his education at the conservatory, where a few academic courses were held. The house was now kept quiet for him so that he could work at the piano undisturbed.

87

Besides these changes, Sonya wanted her son to study with Leonid Nikolaev, and the bustle of these activities did much to keep her mind off of her sorrow. Marusia was graduated that year from her high school, but had still several years ahead of her at the conservatory. Zoya had always been a problem child; her sharp wits and headstrong will resembled her mother's. Besides studying piano like the rest of them, she also took dancing lessons. She was still going to the Stayunin School, but her academic studies did not interest her much, for her whole heart was in her dancing. Her brother Mitya composed for her a "Hopak" and later the *Three Fantastic Dances*. The "Hopak" remained in manuscript, but the *Three Fantastic Dances* were published four years later and became opus 1. These three small pieces have great charm, but show none of the mettle that was to make the Shostakovich of the future. They are obviously written by a boy still influenced primarily by piano compositions; there is an unmistakable flavor of Schumann's *Vogel als Prophet*, and two bars reminiscent of Chopin's Chromatic Étude in A minor, with which Mitya struggled as has every other pianist.

But now there was just not enough money to keep Zoya in her dancing school, and tearfully she had to give it up. Everything was done for Mitya and Marusia, she cried, but nothing for Zoya.

At home the young people were always found with books in their hands, for they were omnivorous readers.

Mitya's favorite author was Gogol; he already began to show interest in Gogol's sharp irony and in the light humor of Krylov, all this much under the influence of his mother. He consulted his mother about all his musical studies as well as his compositions, and it was always to his family that he played his new works first. Nadejda can still remember how falsely he sang his own melodies and how she and Sonya used to tease him about it. He composed at this time two pieces for voice and orchestra on a text of Krylov — *The Dragon-Fly and the Ant*, and *The Jackass and the Nightingale*. Both of these pieces remained in manuscript, and nothing is known of them today.

Through her limitless energy, Sonya secured permission from the conservatory to have a second grand piano in her house. This instrument was given her by a friend. Now they could play all the concerti, either the children accompanying each other or with Sonya as accompanist when she was free. They made many new musical friends and the house resounded with music from morning to night. Now that they had the second piano, Mitya composed a suite for two pianos which he and Marusia played, but which also remained in manuscript.

Their first public appearance together took place early in June 1923, and the placards announcing the performers bore the names of Dmitri and Maria Shostakovich. Besides the Suite for two pianos, Mitya played his own *Three Fantastic Dances* and several compositions by Liszt, including *Gnommenreigen* and the *Don Juan Fantasy*; as an encore he played his *Theme and Variations*. This was one of the first pieces that Mitya composed and is not included in the list of his compositions; those who heard it remember vaguely that the theme was very Russian in character and had ten variations.

Marusia needed a dress for the occasion and there was no money for one. Sonya, however, would let nothing stand in the way of her children's success; she went to work and made her daughter a very handsome gown from her silk bedspread.

With the help of friends, Nadejda and her husband, and Sonya's small earnings, they managed to make ends meet. But the years of undernourishment began to take their toll. Mitya, who had always been pale and delicate, suddenly developed an inflammation of a gland at the side of his neck. Sonya was terrified by these symptoms of the sickness that had killed her little brother Boris and had taken the young life of Lyubochka. She rushed her son to the famous Dr. Grekov, who was an old friend of Dmitri's.

Medical science has proved that tuberculosis germs live everywhere — in the air, in water, in food, in houses, and in the streets. It is not, however, a hereditary disease that can be communicated through the bloodstream. Mitya was born a healthy child, and it is a matter of conjecture whether he caught the germ when he was an infant from his aunt Lyubochka or whether he got it from the milk of a sick cow, from the food, the cleanliness of which was never investigated during the days of hunger, or from his schoolmates. His constitution, made frail by the years of poor nourishment, was fertile soil for the microbes.

So far it had gone no further than inflammation of the cervical gland. Dr. Grekov removed the gland in an operation, but he knew that these glandular inflammations usually come in sequence, and that sometimes the disease spreads, if not checked in time, into the lungs or the bones.

Sonya had known pain and misfortune, and the privations of war and revolution she accepted like a true Russian woman; it was the life of her country and she was ready to bear with it. But the sudden death of her husband and now the first grip of the disease that might cripple or even kill her son, the only hope and meaning in her life, almost threw her into despair.

As humans will, Sonya lashed out at someone near to her; she turned unreasonably on Nadejda, the sister whom she loved. "You," she would say, "you and those like you are responsible for the revolution! And your marriage was complete nonsense. You did it only because you don't love your own family." Nadejda protested, but Sonya would not be stopped.

"If both Mitya and your husband were drowning, which one would you save?" This grossly unfair question always plunged Nadejda into miserable confusion. She would say first: "I would save them both." "No!

No!" Sonya would insist. "Suppose only one could be saved." Nadejda usually ended by saying in tears that she would drown herself.

*   *   *

The fall of 1922 began one of the busiest years for Mitya, for he was to graduate the following spring from his piano class at the conservatory. He was working hard on Beethoven's "Hammerklavier" Sonata. By this time he was a brilliant pianist and the "Hammerklavier" presented no difficulties for him. He spent hours playing for his mother and consulting with her.

The winter of 1922–3 he also worked hard on his compositions. He composed another Scherzo for orchestra, this one in E-flat major, and a Trio for piano, violin, and cello, and he started on a Fantasy, Prelude, and Scherzo for cello and piano. These three compositions were never published. During these months if anyone wanted to present him with anything, he always asked for music paper.

In his class in composition under Steinberg, he met and made friends with other young composers. They gathered together and played their new compositions to each other. On one such occasion one of them played through a symphony he was working on. A few days later, Glazunov met this young composer and said to him: "I like your new symphony very much." The young man was astonished. "But you haven't heard it! I only played it through once a few days ago for the first time," he said. Glazunov replied: "Shostakovich played it for me yesterday."

Both Mitya and Marusia held the famous Glazunov in awe and admiration, and Mitya was very proud of the picture he had of the composer, inscribed: "To my friend." Therefore it was a great occasion for the Shostakoviches when Glazunov accepted an invitation to have tea with them, on the occasion of Mitya's birthday. Sonya, with her usual flair for parties, managed to set her table very attractively with what she had, supplemented by the contents of the package she had received from the American Relief Administration.

Glazunov's weakness for alcohol was well known to everyone, and although there was no wine to be had, Sonya managed to find some vodka for him. Mitya proudly played host and, while keeping his guest's glass filled, he added to his own. Glazunov first proposed a toast to Mitya, and one of the guests immediately followed this with one to the composer of *Scheherazade* — raising her glass and indicating Glazunov. The fact that *Scheherazade* was written by Rimsky-Korsakov did not bother Glazunov in the least, for the toast merely meant to him a chance to have his glass refilled.

Mitya, partly from embarrassment at this mistake and partly from an exaggerated courtesy to Glazunov, was all this time keeping up with his famous guest, glass for glass. It soon became evident that the host was not feeling very well; he was rather green in the face and his mother took him hastily into the music-room.

There he lay throughout the rest of the party with cold compresses on his head. He had for the first time "looked upon the wine when it was red."

*   *   *

In the spring of 1923, after a long and difficult winter, Mitya had to undergo another gland operation. On account of this he missed the regular graduation exercises at the conservatory, and therefore took his graduating examination with others who were also late. The final recital took place in the large hall of the conservatory, which was filled with students, parents and other relatives, and former members of the conservatory. Among the well-known pianists who were listening to that recital was Simon Barer. He says that although the name Shostakovich meant nothing to him at the time, he still remembers the impression the talented young pianist made that day. Dmitri played Beethoven's Appassionata Sonata and a Concert Waltz in D major by Glazunov-Blumenfeld. Barer went backstage afterwards and he remembers that the talk among the professors was mostly of the terrible economic situation in the capital and of the increasing difficulties that the conservatory faced each year; they seemed to feel that art was suffering from the distorted lives that students had to lead in those days. Barer could see for himself the pitiful results in the thin faces and sunken cheeks of the young graduates.

Sonya realized that Mitya needed a long rest and

plenty of sun if he was to pull through the next winter. She decided to send both him and Marusia to the Crimea for the summer. Although Marusia was now twenty and Mitya almost seventeen, they wept like babies at their departure, for they had never been away from their mother before.

This was the last time that Nadejda saw her niece and nephew, for in a week she was leaving with her husband for America. As they parted, Mitya took Nadejda's face in his hands, kissed her, and looked long at her with his light thoughtful eyes.

On the 30th of July, Sonya and Zoya said farewell to Nadejda and her husband, who started on their long voyage to America by way of London. Nadejda threw a little piece of bread on Russian soil as she left — meaning that some day she would return to Russia.

Chapter

6.

"Art happens — no hovel is safe from it, no Prince may depend upon it, the vastest intelligence cannot bring it about." — WHISTLER

AS the waves of the sea take long to subside after the passing of a storm, so the people of Russia, tossed into chaos by the Revolution, had still not found their places in the constantly shifting new life. By 1923 Russia's civil war was over, the last soldier of the foreign army of intervention had left her soil, and the country faced the problem of rebuilding her exhausted and shattered life. Hundreds of thousands of men who had taken off their uniforms and returned to civil life, and as great a number who had lived on the land or in small provincial towns — these, with their families, were moving now into the big cities, all in the hope of finding some work, some means of existence. Many professions had ceased to exist under the new system and thousands who had been petty officials in the government of the old regime were thrown out of employment.

The overcrowded cities did not have sufficient quarters to house them nor was it possible to provide them with jobs. Every available apartment space was requisitioned by the government; families were moved from large quarters into small ones, and strangers were given rooms in apartments that had been occupied by the old tenants for years.

In the early months of 1923 Jasha arrived from Rostov with his wife and three daughters, to see about a position in the Chamber of Weights and Measures, where he had once begun his career, and to look over the prospects of moving from the southern provinces to the capital. He had lived all these years almost exclusively in Rostov. At the beginning of the Revolution he was quite active, but he soon realized that the times had overtaken him; compared with the young revolutionists he had become only a "liberal." He turned back to his interest in invention and devoted his time and energy to serving his country as best he could regardless of politics.

In his late forties Jasha looked like a typical member of the Russian intelligentsia. Though well-built, he had never been particularly good-looking in his youth, but the years had given his features a distinguished aspect. He wore a small beard and his hair was turning gray. During the first years of the Revolution he had overworked and had a stroke which left him with a slight limp. His clothes, though very worn, still preserved their former elegance and he was always very well groomed. He was no longer the *"mauvais ton* Jacques" that he had called himself in his student days, when he had compared himself with his *"bon ton sister"* Sonya.

He came to the capital with a small satchel containing the blueprints of his latest inventions, and the title, bestowed on him by the government, of "Hero of Labor." He used to point out laughingly that one of the special privileges going with this title was a ration card permitting him a cut of cloth suitable for a pair of trousers.

Nadejda managed to find rooms for him in overcrowded Petrograd and asked him if he would mind having two rooms in the apartment of a Communist. "I wouldn't care if it was with the devil himself," replied Jasha; "as a matter of fact, I would rather like it."

His family was just getting acquainted with the city and with their cousins and aunts when Nadejda left for America and both Mitya and Marusia went to the Crimea. Nadejda was glad that Jasha was now in Petrograd and Sonya would not be alone.

It was to a very empty apartment that Sonya and Zoya returned after saying good-by to Nadejda and her husband. Many things had been sold — Nadejda's bed, statuettes and vases, Sonya's astrakhan coat — all to get enough money to make the trip possible for Mitya and Marusia. Glazunov and even Lunacharsky, then Minister of Education, had supplied the young people with letters of recommendation in the hope of getting Mitya free of charge into a sanatorium. But as he could not wait for the letters to come through, the first month had to be paid for and every available ruble was scraped together to keep them alive in the Crimea.

The children were suffering from homesickness so much that Mitya declared he would soon walk home, but Sonya knew that there was not enough money for her to join them, and she was upset at her helplessness in the situation. A couple of old friends moved into the apartment on Nikolaevskaya Street to share expenses and to prevent the requisitioning of rooms for strangers. Sonya took no vacation that summer and the money that she received for her extra time she sent to the Crimea.

Later in the summer she was much distressed to hear that the children had met by chance the same vivacious lady who had taken Lyubochka on her last trip to Germany. This young lady had now chosen to be the patroness of the young Shostakoviches; just as she had managed in Lyubochka's case to get money from friends under the pretext of taking the sick girl to Germany, and then had dropped her in Reichenhall and continued her pleasant trip, so now she proceeded to approach the most influential people in the government, seeking funds in the name of Mitya and his health. The rumor was that she had managed to get from people like Chicherin and Krassin large sums of money; this proved to be true, but it was also true that she kept the money for herself, borrowed an additional sum from Marusia and Mitya, and went off gaily to Berlin.

Sonya was indignant and her pride was hurt in this affair. She felt for the first time the need of a husband to protect the honor of the family. She was angry to think that, after all the sacrifices the family had been forced to make, it might appear that her children's trip was being paid for by the benevolence of this self-appointed patroness. But, above all, Sonya was outraged that her son's name had been used to obtain funds. Even Jasha trusted the young lady's intentions and advised Sonya to send her Mitya's manuscripts. But Sonya refused and was later glad that her intuition had proved to be right.

New projects were being set up throughout Petrograd; jobs would suddenly be available for thousands, and just as suddenly the project would be completed and the thousands would be left again jobless. Healthy youth that could stand privations and endless hours of work had the only chances and Sonya was lucky to be still typing for the Workers' Union. But the staff had lately begun to be reduced, and as even the union itself was in an unstable condition, Sonya's future was uncertain. Nadejda had arranged for her sister to receive the money that had been due to her before she left and also the rest of the food supplies remaining on her academic ration cards, but even this was soon exhausted.

Sonya wrote to Nadejda that she was very tired. The winter was approaching and she must worry about wood. She heard from Mitya that his health was a little better, but everyone was saying that he would need two years in the sanatorium to be cured. There was no money to keep them there for another month, let alone for two years. It was lucky that the second month was free of charge.

Many of Sonya's old friends had left Petrograd; some had gone abroad, some had gone into the provinces hoping to find an easier livelihood and a less hectic existence. There was no place for Sonya and her children to go and she felt deserted and lonely after Nadejda went to America. She was still hurt that her sister had left Russia, not, as she said, to help them all eventually but because Nadejda wanted to follow her husband, because her ideals were different, and because her interest in life was centered on herself. Sonya tormented herself and Nadejda with these reproaches in her first letters to America.

Finally Sonya brought herself to write to Yanovitsky, who since the Revolution had risen to quite an important position, and asked him to help her get a job at the power-house of which he was the head. For a long time Yanovitsky did not answer; then he promised — but nothing ever came of it.

In September Marusia returned to Petrograd, sunburned and six pounds heavier. She was glad to get home, for she had felt all summer that she should be helping her mother. She had left her brother in a sanatorium in Moscow. Though Mitya still had a fever, he had gained thirteen pounds in the Crimea and his stay in Moscow was to be his final rest before resuming work at the conservatory.

Marusia immediately put all of her energy into helping her mother; she soon had a small class of piano pupils and was looking for as many as she could manage. She did the marketing, cooked the meals, took care of the apartment, gave her lessons, and even found time to study herself, for this was her last year at the conservatory.

In November the first American dollar bill arrived; it was for Zoya. Nadejda and her husband had found positions teaching near Chicago and they were going to help the family as soon as they received their first salary.

Mitya played in public several times during the months of November and December. Jasha's daughter Tanya heard her cousin and wrote to Nadejda: "I am in a wild ecstasy about Mitya. I heard him at his concert and he played his compositions. How beautifully he plays! Do you know, one cannot hear him strike the keys. The sounds just grow or fade away. His compositions are very good. Of course, some of them one cannot understand from the first hearing. But others are simple, elegant, and original. It is hard to believe, looking at Mitya, that this boy who is so lively and gay could create such things."

One of Mitya's first professional criticisms, appearing in a *Petrograd* paper, ran as follows:

The concert of the young pianist-composer Dmitri Shostakovich made an excellent impression. He played the Bach Organ Prelude and Fugue in A minor in the Liszt transcription, Beethoven's Appassionata Sonata, and his own works — all with a clarity of artistic intention that showed him to be a musician who deeply feels and understands his art. Shostakovich's compositions, his Variations, Preludes, and *Fantastic Dances*, are fine examples of serious musical thought.

A few days later, he played at the concert of a dancer. Marusia reports: "So long as the ballerina danced alone, there was hardly any clapping; but as soon as she appeared with Mitya (he was to accompany her in his *Three Fantastic Dances*) the hall shook with applause."

The young Dmitri Shostakovich was beginning to have a following.

In his capacity as pianist Mitya appeared in concerts at the conservatory, playing in the Beethoven cycle that was given that winter. And when Professor Nikolaev, who was to play a Bach Brandenburg Concerto under Glazunov's direction, was suddenly taken ill three days before the performance, Mitya was asked to substitute. The young pianist read at sight the concerto at the rehearsal with the orchestra. He also played at the Chamber of Weights and Measures and at the Artists' Club, but all of this brought "no money and no glory," as Sonya put it.

In the first days of December Marusia wrote that her mother was terribly tired from her work, always exhausted and depressed. The cold weather had started and her mother was still going about in her thin coat, for she had no overcoat. She herself, she wrote, was doing all that she could possibly do, but it still was not enough to be of real help.

As Sonya had expected, this year was much harder than the last, when their friends had still been helping them. The faithful Kriftsovs had given what aid they could until one day their house had been broken into and robbed of everything of any value. Jasha had been able to help Sonya occasionally, but he now spent all he earned on his children, who were not well.

Sonya often worked overtime now, trying to get a little extra money, and she came home at eleven or twelve at night, cold and discouraged, and fell exhausted into her bed. She never took a day off; she ate where and when she could, saving every penny for her children. Owing to undernourishment and exhaustion, her body became covered with abscesses. She was advised to rest and to have medical treatment — but how and when could she?

Her friends visited them less and less often; this she expected, for there was so little to offer besides the gloomy depression of her home. The children's spirit was affected by it and Sonya felt that it was somehow all her fault. With an aching heart she saw the three young lives that she had imbued with such high ideals being dulled and crushed beneath the weight of drab necessity.

Sonya's letters to her sister were full of grateful praise of Marusia, who had matured so well under responsibility and who, without a murmur, had taken upon herself the chief support of the family. She was to graduate that spring from the conservatory, and therefore had to snatch what little time she could from her work for her practice. Sonya watched her daughter with a heavy heart. She wanted Marusia to have at least a glimpse of happiness, a little spring in her life, for she had developed into such an attractive young girl. But only Mitya's student friends came to the house, or a few self-styled poets. Sonya wished that Marusia's face could light up at least once with the shy happiness of first love — if not serious, at least a little flirting would make her heart jump and her cheeks flush. The only close friend she had, a young boy by the name of Volodia, was stricken with tuberculosis and lay in bed with a high fever.

The cost of living was rising higher and higher. Since the government, the previous year, had introduced its New Economic Policy and had gone back to free markets, private stores reopened all through the city, goods appeared again in the windows, and with it money came back into circulation in ever increasing flow. Once again rent had to be paid for apartments, and all necessities had to be bought with money one had earned. Only certain commodities, such as fuel and clothing, were rationed at very low prices, but were distributed only among the employees of government offices. Prices in the free markets skyrocketed; average wages could not keep up with the leaps in price. A pair of galoshes cost five billion rubles, while Sonya received for that month's salary three billion. Even foreign currency couldn't keep up with the prices and an American dollar could not buy very much.

In January 1924 Sonya fell ill. Her whole body was in great pain and her temperature went up to 103° and 104°. She stayed in bed for a few days, hoping to shake off the cold she had caught going about in the bitter winter weather with no gloves, no galoshes, and no warm stockings. She was desperately worried about what was going to happen to her children if this sickness should turn into more than a cold — who would take care of them and look after Mitya, who was also sick in bed with bronchitis? She was reconciled to the idea that her life might be over, but she wanted badly to live just so that she might be with her children a little longer.

She fought her way up out of bed and even tried to go back to work; but her temperature rose, she had constant chills in her back, and finally they had to call a doctor. After that she lay in bed for two weeks with malaria and an acute case of exhaustion. Mitya lay in his bed in the next room, his bronchitis keeping him awake all night; his temperature was high and, added to everything else, his glasses were broken and there was no money for new ones. And he was to play a Tchaikovsky concerto at the Home of Scientists on the 20th of January.

While Sonya was in bed she re-read for the first time her correspondence with her husband, Dmitri. The memories it brought back excited and upset her and she got up to write to Nadejda. She wrote of these letters of her husband's, of his love, and of the nobility of his mind and spirit. When she started to read them she had meant to burn them, but now she knew that she could never destroy one page of them. She wanted Mitya to read them, for he, of all the children, had inherited the noble soul of his father, and Sonya wanted desperately for him to be like his father, only happier. She wrote that when she died, she hoped the letters would be buried with her.

As for Zoya, her mother said in despair that she was growing absolutely out of hand. She was lazy and disorderly; she was unpleasant to her mother and to Marusia and seemed to have no appreciation of what her older sister was doing for the family.

A week later Sonya wrote again to Nadejda. She was still in bed; Marusia had just come in and announced that Tanya had received a letter from Aunt Nadejda suggesting that Tanya come to America. Sonya begged her sister to consider seriously having both Marusia and Zoya go too. She had heard that their old friend Frederichs, who had known Nadejda in Göttingen, was going to America and he could take them along and watch over them on the journey. She implored Nadejda to think about it realistically, for their situation was desperate. She had failed to give her children a good life, and perhaps away from home, in a strange country, they would have better luck. She assured her sister that both of her girls could do any work — even manual labor. She herself would stay with Mitya, from whom she could never part; she knew that he would never leave her nor would he ever reproach her for anything.

At the same time Marusia wrote Nadejda after she had gone to see Tanya; the two girls had spent the whole evening discussing the trip to America.

I don't think of anything else but of our trip. I want it so badly. It seems to me I never wanted anything so much in my whole life. Only you must write to me seriously whether I shall be able to find a position — no matter in what capacity. Perhaps as a musician. Couldn't I get a job playing in a movie house, or could I get pupils? Write to me about all of this because I seriously want to come to you, if you have nothing against it. Uncle Jasha told us that we would make the trip from Petrograd to London, and London to New York. . . .

We were worried for a while when we didn't hear anything from you, but the other day Vsevolod Constantinovich [Frederichs] came and read us your letter to him. He will, of course, answer it. Dear Aunt Nadia, please insist on his coming to America, for Mother won't let us go alone. Do you know, I like V. C. more and more every time I see him. He is a real person, a genuine human being in the best sense of the words. He is not like those grimacing and posturing poets and composers that we are surrounded with. Of course, he is no Mitya.

The thoughts of the American adventure were the only bright spot in these dark days, and it was hard to keep the spirit up for long. In her next letter Marusia wrote to her aunt:

Forgive me for writing to you so seldom, but frankly I couldn't write any gay letters now, and I don't want just to upset and disturb you. You know that an unusual sadness and despair lives in our house, and it is all on account of me. I myself have become so strange — I am like a living corpse in the house — an automaton. I work, I teach pupils, I drink, I eat, I sleep, and I am indifferent to everything. If someone visits us I talk and make a gay appearance, but I am really indifferent. Right now, as I write you these things, I know how I disturb you. Please forgive me. I am so miserable, dear Aunt Nadia, I simply cannot go on any longer. I have tortured both Mother and Mitya with my attitude and I still cannot do anything about it. Mother says it is on account of me that our home is like a grave. Yes, it's true. I am so dreadful that there is no happiness for anyone from me. You know, for instance, right now I feel that there is a life that everybody is living, they are all doing something, they are happy or unhappy according to the life they lead — but not I. I am neither one way nor the other. I am like a doll which was put into this life; I look at it and it goes on and on by me and I have no place in it. This is all very stupid; it is not good. I know I should explain all this to you. Mother reproaches me for always being silent and never saying anything, but — would you believe me — I have nothing to say. Mother thinks it might be love, but I have no love — not really being in love. I did have a little flirtation around Christmas, but nothing is left of that except a pleasant memory and right now I am full of depression, terrible depression. It is not from the flirtation — I don't know where it's from. . . .

Do you know that Zenusha, the poor girl, died? It is so strange to receive letters from you asking about her health. And Anochka has a swelling in her brain. The doctor thinks it is a tumor. If that is true, well, then it means that she is going to die. Oh, how horrible! She has been in bed for three months without getting up, and all the time her head aches terribly; and N. Vl. can hardly walk from exhaustion. I am so ashamed that we used to laugh at her.[1] . . .

I will write to you about Mitya and all of us properly next time, in a few days. And now I should give you rest. Don't be unhappy about me, my dear. It will all pass over probably very soon. I love you Aunt Nadia, very, very much and I am terribly unhappy that you are not here. Leave your America and come back to us. I give you endless kisses, I love you.

Yours always,

MARUSIA

PS. My dear Aunt Nadia:

I have a feeling that I am guilty before everyone and you particularly for this letter. So please forgive me and write to me.

But one member of this family, Zoya, seemed to be utterly independent and impatient of the hard neces-

---

[1] Every letter from Russia at this time spoke of the sickness and death of young people — a result of the drastic years of undernourishment.

sity that surrounded them. She was the cause of anger and despair to her mòther and her sister. From her childhood she had always been a problem; she had inherited her mother's stubbornness and strong will, but had met with disappointment very often in her young life. By the time she was ten or eleven years old, the family was already beginning to suffer hardships and what little money there was had always to be spent on Marusia and Mitya.

The fifteen-year-old girl wrote to her aunt:

I love to write letters. I am a great chatterer. This is, of course, a trait that belongs to our weak sex, but it is not usually on such a grandiose scale as it is with me. It seems to me that if I didn't control myself, I would write thousands of pages. Last summer I used to write to one of my friends, and my letters were between sixteen and thirty-two pages and at that I was controlling my passion. This is the week of Palm Sunday. Yesterday I went in the procession after church.[2] This I consider the greatest fun in the world. For a long time I tried to persuade my friends

---

[2] After a church service during the week of Palm Sunday (Pussy Willow Sunday) it was the custom of the worshippers to file out of the church carrying the blessed pussy-willow twigs and a lighted candle. It was a Russian superstition that bad luck would follow if a candle was blown out. The greatest care was taken by everyone on the street to shield his flame so that it would arrive at his house still burning. There was great beauty in the long line of bobbing candles flickering through the dark streets. But spring was in the air during this Holy Week, and the young people were full of mischief. As they drew away from the church they would begin to blow one another's candles out, and it was never long before twigs were whacked on heads and a battle royal was in progress. This battle among the youngsters had come to be almost as traditional as the rest of the ceremony.

to go with me, but they considered that it was "*mauvais ton*" to go there. I used to have a friend who always accompanied me and we used to get into a wild excitement. But she has been for three months in the hospital. She had the measles; she is fifteen years old. And then she had complications in the abdominal glands; and they found pus in the region of her intestines. They have cut the poor thing open three times and once I expected to be told that she had died. It was a miserable time. Now she is much better.

Now, my other friend is a very solid one. She wouldn't take a ride on the merry-go-round or the swing for anything. You see, only children up to twelve go there, and the rest are roughnecks. In the beginning it is a little frightening to approach such gay "attractions"; but after a while one gets into a wild excitement and doesn't remember anything. Do you remember the "American Mountains"? [3] I'll bet you haven't got them in America. I am impatiently waiting for their opening. Soon we shall have Easter, and that means I will go to church. I go to church twice a year — on Thursday and Saturday of Passion Week. I love those services so much; they are remarkably beautiful. You may think that I am very religious and so on. But these days for me are just like going to the theater for the church service is nothing else but theater. All my friends are indignant that I go to church — indignant at my adolescence. But I absolutely don't believe in God and don't go to church to pray but to listen.

Yesterday I visited the Hermitage. [4] I didn't know the Hermitage at all well, so yesterday I devoted a whole day

---

[3] "American Mountains" is the name given by the Russians to the "scenic railways" or "chute-the-chutes" found in amusement parks.

[4] The Leningrad art gallery.

to it. I walked and looked at pictures. I used to be very much against the Dutch school and the German and Flemish; I group them together as German. I couldn't stand Rembrandt or Hals, but yesterday I was convinced to the contrary. I like them very much. I never thought that opinion could change in two or three years to such a degree.

Here I recently received some work to do, and I have earned some money. I am very proud — it is a very pleasant feeling. I wish I could get quickly on my own feet, though I am sure it will never have good results for I have a terribly unrestrained character. I should probably do a lot of silly things. My character hasn't got the slightest stability. Let's take, for instance, art. What haven't I studied? I played the piano, I studied ballet, played the violin, I write verse, and now I am going to sing. Well, it was very hard for me to part with the ballet, but now I am crazy to sing. I was told to go back to ballet, but now I guess I weigh two hundred pounds. Pretty soon I shall be too crowded in my own room. You can't even imagine my immensity! I was given a lot of advice about how to get thin, but nothing had any results. One of the ways is American — to take a newspaper, tear it into little pieces and throw them around the room, and then pick up all the pieces. But I haven't tried this. I am sure that after the first or second piece of paper I should have asthma and might even get an apoplectic stroke. This would be very sad.

I should like, Aunt Nadia, for you to get to know me through these letters and to a certain extent get a picture of what kind of niece you have in the USSR. I will write a little about myself in every letter. Perhaps in this way you will gradually get a clear image of me. Mother and

Marusia race with each other to write you letters, running me down. But I am not such trash as they describe. I am pretty bad, I admit, but still, there are worse. Not often, but there are. I think that in this letter I have written enough about myself. You will have to imagine how immense I am and that is not such a simple job. Well, so that it will be easier for you, I weigh about 130 pounds and am very short. Now please forgive me for this silly letter. The next one will be more clever — with thousands of morals and so on. I don't think it is necessary to write about heart experiences, for they are all clichés. Let this be Marusia's monopoly. But if you should want to know, of course I love a [here Zoya had written the word "fool" and scratched it out] boy. He loves me too and I am contented. I kiss you endlessly.

Your silly,
ZOYA

This is plainly the letter of a young girl who is willful and irresponsible but full of a sense of fun and of imagination. She was undoubtedly going through a phase which might have taken a very different form under different conditions. As it was, one could not expect Sonya to be detached enough to realize this, and so Zoya was a constant source of irritation and pain to her mother.

*　　*　　*

With the help of Nadejda, Marusia's pupils, and Sonya's work, they pulled through the winter. The spring came with warm weather and the approaching summer vacations. Jasha had made plans to go south on a mission for the government, and his family was looking around for a place in which to spend the summer months. Sonya smiled as she listened to her friends' plans for going away and enjoying the good weather, but her heart was heavy, for the summer is the worst time of all for musicians; Marusia's pupils would all be away. Mitya should be sent to the Crimea for a long rest, but everything had been sold that could be sold and there was no one to approach for help.

That spring Sonya thought of a plan about which she wrote her sister. It was to arrange a tour for Mitya as a pianist which would take him through the United States. Sonya would, of course, go with him and leave Zoya and Marusia at home. They could start around April of the next year, 1925, and stay in America up to the fall of that year, until it was time for Mitya to go back to the conservatory, for he still needed two years to finish there. (Apparently Sonya did not realize that the concert season in America closes about April and does not reopen until October.) She wrote that if Nadejda could interest a manager or an orchestra organization, which could invite him to come, and advance the money for the trip, Sonya was sure that they could receive permission from the government to make such a trip. She also was sure that this undertaking would not be risky for any manager, for they could supply a sufficient amount of impressive letters of recommendation from men like Glazunov. As for Mitya, he certainly had a repertoire large enough for many concerts, and his *réclame* would have a solid foundation.

He had been playing all through the winter, but the only time he was paid was when someone had arranged a private concert for him, for which he received a hundred rubles. This sum had to be paid to Zoya's eye doctor. The girl's eyes had been very bad for the last two years. She had developed trachoma and only constant treatment could cure her. But since they could not afford regular treatment, she had not been getting any better. Her illness had recently taken a threatening turn and she was now forced to visit the doctor three times a week; his fee was three rubles a visit. Sonya repeated the old proverb: "Where it is thin, there it tears."

Mitya had grown; he would be eighteen in the fall and he was already taller than Sonya and very good-looking. But he was pale, he had lost four pounds during the winter, and he still ran a temperature. The Home of Science, where he had played recently, liked him very much and arranged for him a free stay at a sanatorium in the Crimea beginning July 15. But there was no money for the trip.

Sonya, however, had to gather together the last remnants of her spirit for Marusia's sake; her daughter was having her graduation examination at the conservatory, and this last year she had had hard work finding time to prepare for the event. But she passed brilliantly and wrote a letter full of happiness to her aunt:

It seems that I finished very well at the conservatory,

and I have been chosen to play at the graduation concert. You cannot imagine how happy I am. Such joy! I am not only a "Free Artist" but also a Laureate of the Leningrad Conservatory! Not bad, is it? You know, I can't think of anything else right now. Frankly, I never expected that this would happen to me. My knees grew weak when I heard about it. The concert will take place day after tomorrow on Sunday the 29th at one o'clock. And I am so excited. Just think, they will write about it in the papers. . . . I dream of getting a position in some school in the fall. That would be so good. Then Mother wouldn't have to work and it would be easier for me not to have to do so much in the house and the kitchen.

When the excitement of the graduation honors had passed, Marusia fell ill. The doctor pronounced it a case of acute anemia and a weakened heart. He also warned them that the work she had done the last year had been too much for her — that she was badly run down, and that if she wasn't taken care of, her lungs might be affected. So Marusia rested that summer and by August she was well enough to play in a concert with a young violinist, Zavetnovskaya. They presented an evening of violin sonatas, and though the hall was not crowded and Marusia received no pay, her name, Maria Shostakovich, appeared on billboards for the first time without her brother's. This bolstered her spirits and her faith in herself. She had not lived for so long among musicians without learning from them that a little success makes them feel that the world belongs to them, and makes them forgive and forget the cruel past.

She thought no longer of going to America; she saw her own life only in connection with her mother and Mitya. She wrote to Nadejda that when Mitya had money she would go with him on a concert tour and that she would "stop off" in America. She had great plans for the future. They were going to travel — "a very enjoyable occupation, especially if one has something to exist on." To see the world would be a great pleasure, but to leave Russia forever — that she could never, never do.

Mitya gave a private concert in July and with the resulting seventy rubles and some borrowed money he went to Gaspra in the Crimea to a sanatorium. But he was back in August, looking just as pale and thin, for he was allowed only one month free of charge. It was then arranged for him to go to the sanatorium of Detskoye Selo (formerly Tsarskoye Selo) providing they could pay fifty rubles a month. The seemingly impossible was arranged, in spite of the fact that through the reduction of the staff at the Workers' Union Sonya had finally lost her job.

Jasha was away on a business trip for the government; he was well paid for this, but was in no position to help Sonya, for he had sent his family to a small village on the border of Finland. Jasha's children enjoyed themselves there much in the manner Sonya's had in Irinovka, lying in the sun, bathing, and playing in the woods, getting back the strength they had lost through the dark winter days of Leningrad, which they had hated. Under their mother's direction, they organized plays, using Red Army men in their casts, and performed with such success that they were invited to the neighboring villages. They wrote glowing accounts of their summer to their cousins in Leningrad, and asked them to come and join them. But for Sonya there was sad irony in these invitations, since her family that summer was eating only one meal a day. On Zoya's sixteenth birthday there was not a kopeck in the house and her mother only hoped that later they might be able to get her "a little something sweet to eat."

The winter of 1924-5 found the Shostakoviches facing the same bitter fight for existence that they had known before. Marusia managed to obtain the position of music-teacher in a ballet school, the First Academic Government Theater School, which was back of the Alexandrovsky Theater. Here she was to teach from nine in the morning to three in the afternoon, and two evenings a week. This was a refreshing atmosphere for Marusia; the staff consisted mostly of people who had been there for years, and Marusia, being young, handsome, and a Laureate of the conservatory, was treated with affection and respect. The staff admired her and the children lost their hearts to her.

At three Marusia took her half-hour walk home and from four to seven and sometimes to nine she gave her private lessons. But she was happier than she had been for a long time. Her salary, though small, provided her with the steady income that her family was much in need of. Sonya had looked for a long time for another job (as she said, "Jobs were easy to lose and hard to get in those days") and had finally been given one as substitute cashier in the store of the Workers' Union. Her hours were from nine in the morning till ten at night and she received hardly anything for her work.

Their debts were more than they could ever hope to catch up with. Even with Nadejda's help, they had had to borrow last spring, then again in the summer for Mitya's sanatorium payments. They had not paid the rent for months, and they were being sued for the piano; it had once been given to them — and now suddenly they were asked to pay the large sum of 250 rubles for the past use of it.

Sonya had written her sister the spring before that Mitya was in disgrace at the conservatory. Even Jasha had heard of it and made the wry comment: "Mitya seems to be making progress with his music; the symptoms of this lie in the fact that the Leningrad musicians are pecking at him. Until now they haven't given him a proper chance to have a concert."

A group of students headed by two whose names were Schmidt and Renzin had voted Mitya out of the Academy and he was officially considered expelled from his piano class at the conservatory. The same group of students with the backing of the authorities wanted to suspend the scholarship given by Glazunov, of eight rubles each winter month; but Glazunov, since it was a gift in his own name, prevented this.

At the same time Mitya missed his chance to play with the Philharmonic Orchestra. They had wanted him to play the Tchaikovsky concerto, but had to have an official statement from the boy's professor, Nikolaev, that he had listened to him play it through and that Mitya was ready for the performance. This audition would take an hour out of Nikolaev's schedule, but the authorities in the conservatory, ignoring Nikolaev's personal affection for his pupil, never found time for Mitya to play the concerto for him. Mitya's lessons were given him by Nikolaev free of charge, and so whenever Nikolaev had an hour to spare, the conservatory assigned the time to someone who was paying.

Mitya was seriously upset over the affair. He grew paler and lost weight; his temperature jumped. Sonya was most concerned over the effect of these intrigues on her son's health, and in her letters did not speak of the real reason for them, but one could guess that it was not because he did not lift his fourth finger high enough. Mitya did not belong to any party, nor did Sonya; and Sonya had lost her job partly on account of it. It was clear that Mitya's position in the conservatory during this winter was only tolerated; the conservatory had promised to settle the matter of the piano, which had been dragging on for months, but nothing was done and the piano was carried out of the house. Apparently the "bourgeois past" of the Shostakovich family still hung over their heads. But Sonya never explained it in her letters, and journalists and music-critics today prefer to spin fairy tales like the following:

One day many years ago, a students' delegate came to the director of a certain educational institution and said: "Our city is going through a very difficult time along with the rest of the country and we know this. We know too that the limited resources and provisions remaining after five years of war fought on Russia's fields must be distributed primarily among those who are defending the young Republic. Nevertheless, we are asking you to include one young student from the conservatory in the list of those who, having shown outstanding abilities in science and art, are guaranteed special rations in accordance with instructions issued by the government and Comrade Lenin personally."

The director of the conservatory, a composer whose name is known all over the world, decided the question very promptly. "Academic rations are not, of course, intended for youngsters of thirteen, but this is an exceptional case. This boy's gifts are phenomenal, comparable to Mozart's. He is the future of our music. I would willingly give up my own rations in his favor, if they cannot find sufficient for him."

That was at the Petrograd Conservatory in 1919, when its director was Alexander Glazunov. The thirteen-year-old boy of whom they were speaking was Dmitri Shostakovich.[5]

Not only are these statements completely inaccurate, but they reflect most unfavorably on Glazunov's mu-

---

[5] From an article by D. Rabinovich and S. Schlifstein, written on the occasion of Shostakovich's Seventh Symphony and cabled to America in 1942.

sical judgment. When Dmitri was thirteen he was still, as the reader knows, a pupil of Mme Rozanova; he had composed only a few little pieces, which still remain in manuscript. There was therefore no basis whatsoever for Glazunov's comparing him to Mozart. And five years later, when Mitya had actually become a brilliant pianist and tried desperately to get the engagement with the orchestra — where was Glazunov then?

Not knowing what the "precious privileged ones" would think of next, Sonya wrote to Moscow, thinking to get Mitya completely away from Leningrad, and tried to get an opportunity for him to study there. But even had she succeeded in this, it would have broken up their lives and played havoc with their finances.

When Mitya came back in the fall from the sanatorium and saw again the distress his family was in, he took his own steps.

"Our greatest misery," writes Marusia to her aunt Nadejda in October, "is that Mitya is going to play in a movie house. This is a real tragedy for us, considering the hard work and his health. But he says that he cannot stand our life any longer and will feel much better if he could bring home some money every month." Mitya passed the audition qualifying him for this job and so began his work in the movies. To Sonya this was a bitter blow — that her son, an artist, should be reduced by poverty to being a hack player in a movie house; but her chief worry was the drain of this work on her son's health.

The little theater was old, drafty, and smelly; it had not seen fresh paint or a scrubbing brush for years, the walls were peeling, and the dirt lay thick in every corner. Three times a day a new crowd packed the small house; they carried the snow in with them on their shoes and overcoats. They munched food that they brought with them, apples and sunflower seeds that they spat on the floor. The heat of the packed bodies in their damp clothes, added to the warmth of two small stoves, made the bad air stifling hot by the end of a performance. Then the doors were flung open to let the crowd out and to air the hall before the next show, and cold damp drafts swept through the house.

Down in front below the screen sat Mitya, his back soaked with perspiration, his near-sighted eyes in their horn-rimmed glasses peering upwards to follow the story, his fingers pounding away on the raucous upright piano. Late at night he trudged home in a thin coat and summer cap, with no warm gloves or galoshes, and arrived exhausted around one o'clock in the morning.

But even with Mitya's help there seemed to be very little hope of keeping a roof over their heads. They had not paid the rent for months and their creditors were suing them. They had received notice that their belongings were to be appraised and sold for debts.

It was in the midst of this that Mitya began composing his First Symphony.

* * *

In the middle of November Sonya sat on her cashier's stool in the Workers' Union and wrote a letter to her sister Nadejda. She was working at that time thirteen hours a day; the bitter cold of the Leningrad winter penetrated the room and she wrote that she never had a chance to thaw out until she got home at night. She hardly saw her children at all, she said, except late at night just before they all went to bed. She wrote that she still hoped that a tour could be arranged for Mitya that would take them out of the nightmare they were living in.

But when this letter arrived in America, it was enclosed in a letter from Marusia dated three days later. Marusia wrote:

I am enclosing a letter Mother wrote you from the store. That night when Mother came home she was almost killed by a robber who had probably followed her from the store, thinking she had money on her. This happened at half past ten at night. Mother was already on the staircase, which was very well lit, when suddenly a young man approached her and it seemed to her as though he shot at her. She moved toward him, crying: "Who are you? What do you want?" Here she felt something drip on her hand and she saw it was blood. The blow she had received was so terrific that there had been sparks in her eyes and she had taken those sparks to be the flash of a revolver. But he had not shot at her, he had hit her with something made of metal — for later, in the hospital, they said that such a blow could not have been inflicted with a wooden stick. As soon as Mother realized that she was wounded, she began to ring the bells of all the apartments on that floor, crying out that she had been hit and begging someone to open a door. But no one did. Then she fell down and when she later came to she screamed. This was heard by Zoya (who was on the fifth floor); she ran downstairs and saw Mother's face and hands covered with blood and, frightened to death, she helped Mother. Both Mitya and I were out. Zoya fetched Ismailova, who washed Mother's wound, put an ice-pack on her head and called Mme Grekov's husband, who is a surgeon. He came at once and looked at Mother. Luckily the bones were intact. The next day I took Mother to the hospital, where they wanted to take stitches, but it was too late and so they just bandaged her. All this happened on Wednesday the 19th of November. Fortunately, Mother is alive. The wound is terrible — her whole head is cut, the part is bloody, and the skin around the temple is torn. It looks ghastly. Of course we were terrified. Today Mother feels a little better and she even got up. . . . If he wanted to rob her, why didn't he grab her muff? But he didn't touch anything. We even think it might have been a madman, or perhaps he mistook her for someone else. But he definitely wanted to kill her.

One more misfortune awaited the family in this year that had been so hard for them. Late in December someone stole a hundred rubles out of Sonya's cash register. Besides being a financial catastrophe, for they had no money to pay it back, Sonya's honesty was involved and she tried desperately to find the money to repay the loss. She was never accused of the theft, but a month later she lost the job.

However, the family's decision to remain where they were never wavered. During the two years that Nadejda had been in America, the letters from Russia always implored her to come home. How could one stay away from one's country forever? "I cannot understand," writes Zoya, "how a Russian could live in America. There is no real life, no real human beings. They are all just machines. They don't have our Russian verve and they have no art and no talents. Over America hangs the genius of materialism. What good is it that the industries are well developed and full of economic wealth? What is all this when there is no life? I couldn't live there a week. I pity you, Aunt Nadia, terribly. There is no better land in the world than our Russia. There is nothing better than Leningrad. For in America there is no poetry. Take, for instance, this: They are fixing our street, and the sign-post for the trolley was removed. So they stuck a wooden stick in a barrel and wrote on it "Trolley Stop." Now, isn't that delightful? What a lot of poetry there is in that — it is so touching! They say that in America to see a horse on the street is a rare occurrence. Of course, I am wildly in love with Leningrad and couldn't even imagine a better city."

By January 1925 Marusia was once more the sole support of her family. For shortly after his mother lost her job, Mitya was forced by his health to give up his. Marusia wrote: "We are again in a panic. Mitya has another mean swelling on his neck. But a few days ago

Mother put a new collar on Mitya's shirt and that may have caused the swelling because the skin on his neck is so tender." This meant a hospital, an operation, doctors, and long treatments — and above all a steady, healthful regime, which he could not have until he went into a sanatorium in the spring, and spring was far away. But it was imperative that he stop working at the theater immediately. Marusia wrote that she wished she herself could shoulder all this pain and sickness instead of Mitya. They had to worry about every step he took, everything he did, fearing that one slip might be fatal. An acquaintance of theirs — a girl of about the same age as Mitya — had the same swellings, which had spread all over her body; she was now lying in the hospital with peritonitis and the doctors had pronounced her case hopeless. This picture haunted both Marusia and Sonya.

Sonya went from office to office looking for work, but was refused everywhere. She who was so used to sacrificing herself to keep her children alive was losing her spirit. Neither hunger nor cold had been able to destroy the hope that some day they would pull out of their misery; but now that she was turned down everywhere she trudged home beaten and bowed by her misfortune. She walked slowly because she hated to see the apartment, where there was neither tea nor bread and where she had to face her children and tell them that she had failed. She felt that her life was finished, that no one wanted the little strength she had left to save her children from hunger. She wrote again to Yanovitsky, asking him to help her find work, but he didn't answer, and the help that came from Nadejda just wasn't enough. Jasha did what he could, but none of these small bits could pull them out of their depths. Besides, Sonya did not want the everlasting borrowing, the humiliating begging for help. She had been writing letters of this kind for over a year and now her hand refused; the once proud woman had come to the end of her humility. She wanted a job no matter how hard it was and no matter how little it paid. Since she was not working, she felt that she had no right to take bread away from her children. Was she, then, she cried to her sister, to go on the street and beg?

Jasha was doing his utmost to get her into the Chamber of Weights and Measures, where her husband had worked for so long, and where he had been so well liked that there was a portrait of him hanging in the office. But this took patience and time and the poor cannot afford to wait. Sonya wrote to her sister that she thought of taking her life. She even thought of ending the lives of her children — in fact, she told them about it, and they spoke of it in the calm way one decides to take a trip or a long-wanted rest.

By February it became certain that Marusia had tuberculosis; but the family was dulled to shock and accepted this new misfortune almost with resignation. What bitter irony it was for Sonya to have to listen and smile while Nikolaev told her that Mitya was becoming a really fine pianist and that one should begin to think of his career! Now was the time, he said, for Mitya to start concertizing. But the young pianist was still being pushed aside by the Leningrad musicians and he did not play anywhere all that winter. To begin a concert career, even in Russia, one needed a large sum of money or else a pull with the powers that be, and Sonya knew no one.

She still had not given up the idea of a tour of America, but a letter from Nadejda proved that her sister was unable to do anything to help them. Nadejda, who was not very familiar with the machinations of American concert managers, had approached Ossip Gabrilówitsch after a concert of the Detroit Symphony Orchestra which he had conducted in Ann Arbor. She told him of her nephew and of the situation he was in, and showed him Glazunov's letter of recommendation. Gabrilówitsch, whose dressing-room was crowded with friends who had come to congratulate him, scanned briefly Glazunov's letter and handed it back to Nadejda with the words: "I have dozens of letters brought to me asking me to help people — I can't do anything for them." With this, he turned smilingly to one of his patronesses and left Nadejda alone. Nadejda wrote her sister that she thought Mitya's best chance in America would be as a teacher. Sonya replied that he did not have any talent for teaching, but that if he did choose it she hoped that he would be offered a professorship in the Leningrad conservatory. In any case, he would never leave Russia for long; he worshipped his country and considered himself bound to it. "It is amazing," Sonya wrote, "how early in his youth he understood the aims of the Bolshevik Revolution, and how deeply he considers himself a part of them."

But the discouraging news from Nadejda was accompanied by the generous sum of ninety-six rubles. This was a godsend to the family and they were able to catch their breath for the first time in months. Sonya paid the two months' rent for the last year that they still owed; the rest of it went to pay doctors and old debts, and they had just enough left to buy a quarter of a pound of tea, some sugar, and two bars of Mitya's favorite chocolate.

A position finally opened for Sonya at the Chamber of Weights and Measures; it was only a part-time job, but with it came the promise that eventually she would have a full-time one with much better pay. She also gave a piano lesson twice a week.

In the spring Mitya graduated from his composition class at the conservatory and as his final work he submitted his First Symphony, which he had just finished. In spite of the opposition to him that still existed, the symphony was well received and his family hoped that it would be played. But the parts had to be copied and for this Mitya needed 150 rubles. Those 150 rubles, however, if they could be scraped together, would have to be used for whatever cure could be managed for the two sick children that summer.

*　　*　　*

Two years had passed since Jasha moved to Leningrad. His work had earned him honors and respect, and an ample income to supply his family with a fairly good living. But the work was hard, and constant worrying over his children's health and over the future, which was never very certain even for a man in his position, began to tell on his health. In frank conversation with Sonya he sometimes admitted how light-hearted his children were, how little prepared they were to take care of themselves. But apparently he did not press them to get on their own feet and was delighted with the small progress that they were making.

This spoiling of Jasha's children frightened Sonya; of course it was all right so long as Jasha was earning so much money and they could eat and live as they did, but God knew what would become of all of them if anything should happen to Jasha. Sonya felt that her brother was not appreciated in his home and that he was being treated rather like a pack-horse.

In the spring of 1925 Jasha had a stroke. The Chamber of Weights and Measures was very considerate and provided him with special medical treatment and, later on, with the means to take a carriage to and from his office. The doctors found his health fundamentally still sound and believed that with care he would eventually be completely well again.

Jasha planned to move to Detskoye Selo, where they

could have a house with a small yard and a vegetable garden. They spoke of it constantly and had already invited Mitya and Marusia to come and spend the summer there, where his wife Nina would feed them all on the products from their own garden.

But the summer found them still in their old two rooms in the city, and Detskoye Selo with the chickens and the vegetables remained a dream.

To the great surprise of everyone, Zoya graduated from her high school. She spent the summer alone with her mother, for Mitya and Marusia had gone to visit friends in Oranienbaum. Sonya and her daughter did not cook one warm meal for themselves that summer. Occasionally they called in a Tatar peddler from the street and sold him whatever he would take from what was left in the apartment, for a couple of rubles — sometimes for only fifty kopecks. That meant another meal — another day of life for them. Sonya still wore her old suit, which was too hot for the summer, and her one change of linen was falling to shreds on her back. She was losing her front teeth and her legs were swelling from standing eight hours a day in the shop. Once when she visited Jasha, he was so upset by her appearance that he gave her fifteen rubles so that she could get a few things for herself. But Sonya sent them to Mitya and Marusia.

That winter the family went back to its familiar drudgery. Marusia resumed her work at the ballet school and Sonya, in addition to her own job, took over some of Marusia's lessons, for Marusia had to teach some fifty pupils in the school and her health was growing steadily worse. To make ends meet and pay the debts of the summer, Mitya had to go back to his playing in the moving-picture theater. Jasha could no longer help them, for he had had a second stroke and was very ill. "Sonya's affairs are very bad," he wrote. "I wish I could help her more than I occasionally do . . . they live on Marusia's earnings, Sonya's small salary, and whatever Mitya can make. But it is not enough for the four of them. . . . If only something will come out of Mitya!"

The only ray of hope was that the conservatory had undertaken the expense of having the parts copied from the score of Mitya's symphony; Nikolai Malko, then the conductor of the Leningrad Philharmonic, was studying the score. That winter of 1925–6 Sonya clung to her job; she brought very little money home, for she was still paying off the hundred rubles that had been stolen from the cash register. Marusia worked all day long giving lessons at the ballet school, and Mitya resumed his job at the moving-picture house. But even so, they still had no warm things to wear and no sweets to eat; they could not afford butter and used only the cheapest grease. They almost never went out, since they had no good clothes and could not afford to go to a theater. They went only to the Philharmonic concerts, where Mitya had free entrance. Jasha had once written about his sister: "Sonya, the damn fool, just received her first few rubles of salary and of course immediately sank the whole amount in a festival for her kids; now they subsist on the food of St. Anthony"; but in these days Jasha could no longer reproach her for such foolishness.

During that winter Mitya was sent, at the government's expense, to Moscow as a representative of Leningrad's modern composers. Moscow received him very well; he was fêted wherever he went, and it was promised that his compositions would be published after the performance of his First Symphony. His Octet for strings and his *Three Fantastic Dances* for piano would be published along with the symphony. On his return to Leningrad a definite date was finally set for the performance of the symphony — the 8th of May 1926; it would be played under the direction of Nikolai Malko. But Sonya heard unofficially through friends that there was still opposition to Mitya and to the performance, and they were worried for fear something else would be substituted on the program.

A breath of fresh air blew into the apartment on Nikolaevskaya Street with the arrival of their cousin Shura Zakonov, who had come from Siberia and visited with the family for a few days. He was a husky young man of twenty-five, red-cheeked and cheerful, who had, as Sonya said, "a very philosophical outlook on life." He was bursting with health and next to him Mitya looked like a ghost; Sonya's heart contracted when she saw them together. "Such a Siberian!" wrote Marusia.

"He is married; his wife is older than he; she is twenty-six and, according to her photograph, not very beautiful. Oh well, happiness does not lie in looks."

Sonya listened with a faint pang of jealousy to her nephew's account of how his family lived; his parents had rented a large house and they and their married children all lived together in easy congeniality. Sonya remarked later that the samovar was apparently never off the table and that Dr. Zakonov might have got further in his medical career if he had not surrounded himself with this slovenly and chatty atmosphere. Sonya wanted people to *do* things and was intolerant and critical of long-winded chatter.

At the end of January Mitya received the orchestra parts of his symphony to be corrected. It was such "hellish work," as Mitya said to Marusia, that he doubted that he would ever be finished with it. He was still playing in the theater, and in the spare time that he managed to find he was practicing Chopin Études, Schumann's *Carnaval* and Liszt's *Don Juan Fantasy*, which were to be in the program of his next concert whenever that happy event should occur.

"Mother is sick now," wrote Marusia; "she has sciatica, which is so painful; there are days when she actually cannot get up or sit down or turn around. Zoya is the only one who is still raging and we are all terrified of her. She doesn't want to do a thing. It is not so bad now, but later — one should never depend on anyone but oneself, and should, I think, before everything, make oneself independent."

But Zoya felt more than her family would give her credit for. "Everyone at home is working, I am the only one who does nothing. Once in a while, in a burst of anger, Marusia will say that I am not doing anything and am eating her bread — and the words just scald me."

But Zoya's pride and spirit didn't keep her down for long and she continues in her usual vein: "But then, with Olympian calm, I put on my coat and go to drown myself in the Neva. But nothing ever comes of it. Either the Neva is frozen, or I meet somebody I know on the way and so am forced to put it off. Now I have discovered a new way of warding off the blows of fate — I write verse. It is very easy and soothes the nerves wonderfully."

The following spring, on the 12th of May, the First Symphony of the eighteen-year-old Dmitri Shostakovich was given its first performance. A week later Sonya wrote her sister that she was ill and too tired to write her a long letter and so was enclosing a copy of a letter that she had written to her old friend Clavdia Lukashevich. She wrote:

My dear Clavdia Vladimirovna:
I will try to describe to you our feeling of excitement in connection with the performance of Mitya's symphony. All winter long we lived only for this happy day, and as

the time drew closer our thoughts, our conversation, and our wishes all centered more and more on it. The posters appeared on the billboards two weeks before. Mitya was counting the days and the hours. He had been in a state of great excitement, wondering whether the parts had been correctly copied, whether he had orchestrated well, and how it would all sound. At last came the 10th of May, the day of the first orchestral rehearsal. (The symphony had been postponed to the 12th of May because on the 8th *Salome* was being given at the Mariinsky Theater and the brasses that we need for our symphony were occupied there.)

Working in my office all day long, I hardly heard or understood a thing — I was only waiting for the telephone. About three o'clock I heard at last Mitya's happy little voice: "Everything sounds — everything is all right!" The orchestra and those who were present at the rehearsal gave Mitya his first ovation. I myself went to the second rehearsal on the 11th of May (I managed to get away from my job). I heard all the glowing praise given to Mitya's talent by everyone with musical authority. Glazunov told me that he was particularly amazed by Mitya's mastery of orchestration — something that is usually acquired only with years of technical experience but which shone forth so brightly in this first composition for large orchestra. Again there was praise — an ovation, and Mityusha's happy little face.

At last came the day of the concert — the 12th of May. The excitement began in the early morning. Mitya hadn't slept — and he didn't eat or drink. I was afraid to look at him. At half past eight in the evening we dressed and went to the Philharmonic. By nine o'clock the concert hall was filled. What I felt when Malko came out on the

stage and picked up his baton would be hard to describe
to you, my dear. . . . I can only say that even a great
happiness is sometimes hard to live through. . . .

All went more than brilliantly — a splendid orchestra
and magnificent execution! But the greatest success went
to Mitya. The audience listened with enthusiasm and the
scherzo had to be played twice. At the end Mitya was
called to the stage over and over again. When our handsome young composer appeared, looking almost like a
little boy, the enthusiasm turned into one long thunder-
ous ovation. He came to take his bows, sometimes with
Malko, sometimes alone.

After the concert, there was a great festival at the Shostakoviches', at which were present almost exclusively the
representatives of the musical world — Malko, Nikolaev,
Steinberg; Glazunov did not come (but he was at the concert); he has been sick with glandular trouble and our
fifth-floor climb is too strenuous for him. When Mitya
and Malko arrived, Nikolaev and Steinberg played Glazunov's Fanfare on the piano and cheered him. The party
was very modest, but the food was tasty — there was
enough of everything — and the guests departed at five
o'clock in the morning.

Mitya received from Nikolaev three finely bound books
on Scriabin, with a touching inscription. The painter Ko-
stenko sent him an engraving, and from different friends
came presents of an ice-cream freezer, two peach tarts, a
bottle of champagne from Sukachov, two bottles of wine,
oranges and apples. His aunt Marusia [wife of Kostrykin]
sent him ten rubles. Mikhail Mikhailovich Kucherov
wrote verses for the toasts, which were read during supper.
I am sending them to you with this letter — and also some
comical ones which were written before the performance.

DMITRI SHOSTAKOVICH

A big house on a Leningrad street
Is the Shostakovich family seat.
The family center — its head and heart —
Is the gallant mother — with whom we start.

She's a simple woman with a noble soul;
She works in the Union all day long.
She cranks the cash-box and the rubles roll,
And no matter how tired, she does nothing wrong.

She has two daughters — two bright stars —
Whom we hope no misfortune ever mars.
Marusia, the elder, is always busy;
She runs back and forth until she's quite dizzy.

Early in the morning she runs to her school
And works there till three, for that's the rule.
Then runs home again, no rest to enjoy,
And her poor head aches and she sighs, Oy, Oy!

Then swarms of pupils she must teach
To make their little fingers reach
O'er scales and trills and Bach and Liszt —
With "Sit up straight" and "Drop your wrist";
And all this noise each neighbor hears
And vainly tries to stop his ears.

Zoya, the youngest, is the family storm;
She won't have peace in any form.
She roars from her corner in a voice like thunder
That splits the ceiling and the walls asunder.
And if she is scolded — she will defy it.
The library's the only place Zoya is quiet.

This family has an idol — a little god —
Who conquers the world with a magic rod.
His mighty talents will keep him from perdition —
This is Mitya, our young musician.

Oh Mitya drinks and Mitya smokes,
And Mitya plays concerts for the folks.
His musical friends and he play chess —
A very versatile group, we stress.

Now Mitya would like to fall in love,
But he doesn't dare — by the gods above! —
For, being a simple young musician,
Mitya's afraid of competition.

But to his house comes every day —
Hoping he will look her way —
A modest widow, neat and trim,
Who seems to be in love with him! [6]

* * *

"We were at the concert," wrote Jasha's wife, "and listened to Mitya's symphony — very original, full of the most unexpected transitions; I am inclined to think it is a difficult one to understand from the first hearing. Mitya orchestrated it with great mastery and it was a great success. Mitya was called out over and over again."

Tanya added her own note to her mother's letter:

The criticisms of Mitya's symphony are very good. They say he is exceptionally talented — a genius, remark-

---

[6] Free translation by Katherine Seroff.

able orchestration — but personally I didn't particularly like it. Of course, I am a complete layman in music — although I love it. Mitya played the symphony for us at our house on the piano, and of course it sounded all different from the way it came out in the orchestra. In many places one is overwhelmed with a lot of beautiful sounds, but in some places it is very empty — strained. There is a place in the second movement where the orchestra plays a crescendo going to forte and then suddenly breaks and here the piano comes in with a scale — or whatever it is called — just very fast up and down the whole of the keyboard. After the orchestra, the piano sounds like a mosquito. This place struck my nerves; it was as though someone jerked me and woke me up. I am sure that if a connoisseur heard me talk he would say that I don't understand anything. And of course I would agree with him. . . .

You know, Mitya has suddenly changed from an adolescent into a young man. He has grown much taller. Aunt Sonya is very upset that Mitya, up to now, hasn't paid court to the girls. As for me, I understand this — he is so awkward; but this only proves that he has such an unspoiled nature. What will happen to his talent? Will he be appreciated or will he be acclaimed only after his death, like so many composers? His music does not sound contemporary to me; the only music that is praised today is full of dissonances that hurt your ear and not the powerful harmonies in the major key as it is with Mitya. But there is no point in guessing ahead. The future will show itself.

When later Nadejda heard the First Symphony in America, the melodies reminded her of those in *The*

Dragon-Fly and the Ant, which Mitya had composed in 1922 and which he used to play to his family. According to Nadejda, the themes from this composition as well as his early Scherzo were used in his First Symphony. In the first movement, she says, one hears the recitative of the flighty, irresponsible dragon-fly and the mutterings of the laboring ant. Then comes a march of all the insects, with the fireflies leading the way; they range themselves in a semicircle in the amphitheater and the dragon-fly performs a dance on the stage. The Scherzo is inserted in full. In the last movement, the second theme for violin and cello is taken from an unfinished piece that Mitya was composing at the time of *The Dragon-Fly and the Ant*; he was writing it around Andersen's story of the Mermaid, an idea that had been suggested to him by his mother. With the last movement of the symphony, Nadejda remembers how Mitya described to his family the Mermaid swimming up through the waters of the lake to the brightly lit castle where the Prince is holding a festival.

*   *   *

Mitya's symphony was presented at the last concert of the Leningrad Philharmonic, and with it the musical season was over.

A couple of months later Mitya made his debut in Moscow — an event which turned into a sort of Shostakovich festival. The Moscow *Evening Radio*, reviewing the second symphony concert, said:

Without discovering an America, without pursuing any new combinations of sounds, the young composer Shostakovich made his debut with his First Symphony. It is a symphony which reflects all that a composition can give of the most important in the artist. . . . The first steps of the composer are significant.

Reviewing the third symphony concert, the same paper stated:

Shostakovich, who made his debut with Tchaikovsky's concerto, has shown the other side of his talent. At the piano sat a musician, already mature, who possesses rich qualities based on a solid foundation. The conclusion drawn from these two appearances as composer and as pianist is that the absence of the great leaders of our music who have emigrated abroad, doesn't frighten us. They have successors.

After these two appearances Mitya gave his own concert, in which he played many of his own compositions.

The second part was entirely devoted to Liszt, a task which came off brilliantly. One rarely hears such a profound and universal treatment of Liszt's compositions. An easy mastery of technique and a masterly use of Liszt's palette. Shostakovich does not lose himself in plain virtuosity, but gives a performance full of poetry. The pathos of the sonata, the monumental build-up of the *Funerailles*, the tenderness of the Canzonetta, and the boiling upsurge of the Tarantella — all these were equally successful in the pianist's hands. Shostakovich belongs, without a doubt, to our most outstanding interpreters.

Isvestia, Russia's leading paper next to *Pravda,* praised the First Symphony and added: "The First Symphony is almost classical." The reviewer Anton Uglov concluded: "However, it will be unfortunate if Shostakovich should cultivate, in the future, purely academic music. His qualities, without doubt rich, give him the responsibility of lifting himself to the higher and broader social themes of our epoch."

The summer brought the same old story for the Shostakovich family — Marusia's work stopped and Mitya's health needed attention — the same *"perpetuum mobile,"* as Sonya wearily called it, from which there seemed to be no escape. The symphony was to be published the following winter and perhaps then would bring in its first material rewards.

But meanwhile even the small help from Nadejda stopped. For the past two and a half years she had been sending Sonya whatever she could spare from salary for her work, first at the Goertner Scientific Corporation in Chicago and then as assistant at the University of Michigan. But now that Jasha's illness had taken so grave a turn, both Nadejda and her husband were giving what help they could to the Kokaoulin family.

By June of 1926 Jasha's case was pronounced hopeless and his wife was told by the hospital authorities to take him home. The last kopeck had been used up during the three months of hospital treatment and the family was deeply in debt. Tanya had to give up her dreams of being a singer; she applied for work at the

Chamber of Weights and Measures, the only place where her name was well known. Her only credentials were the fact that her father had worked there for twenty-five years and had been honored with the title of Hero of Work and Science. Tanya needed these facts to back up her application, for in those days strong preference was given to those of proletarian background or to those who were members of the Communist Party; the Kokaoulin family had neither of these requirements. Sonya did what she could for them; she forgot her criticism and disapproval of the way Jasha had brought up his children and did her best to help them get jobs. Meanwhile she even managed to give them an occasional five or ten rubles.

Jasha had sclerosis of the brain, brought on largely by physical and mental exhaustion. For six months he lay in bed, a helpless invalid, and on the 26th of February 1927 he died. After his burial the family was in desperate need of funds and, through Sonya's endeavors, it was arranged that a collection be taken up at the Chamber of Weights and Measures. This amounted to 180 rubles, which went for doctor's and medical bills and left them with enough to go on for a while.

*　　*　　*

While the two families were absorbed in Jasha's last illness, Mitya was in Poland. Under the auspices of the Polish government, an International Piano Contest was arranged in Warsaw to celebrate the unveiling of the Chopin Monument. The greatest exponents of the pianistic art as well as the most famous teachers of piano were appointed judges. The music was to be only Chopin's, and young pianists from all over the world came to Warsaw to take part in the competition. Besides the monetary rewards, the prize-winners had the opportunity of playing with the Warsaw Philharmonic, this providing them with a brilliant opening for a career.

The Soviet Government decided to send among others young Dmitri Shostakovich, and Mitya was notified, only two weeks before the event. He had to work very hard, for he had to learn anew many Chopin compositions, "some hundred and fifty-eight pages," according to Nina. He played his program with the other Russian competitors at the Moscow Conservatory and at the Polish Embassy before they left for Warsaw, and had great success.

But Mitya did not win a prize at the competition; he came away only with a diploma of honorable mention. From Warsaw he went, at the expense of the Soviet Government, to Berlin, where Bruno Walter was to conduct his First Symphony. "Mitya begins to emerge in the musical world," wrote his Aunt Nina, "and *only* through his talent."

Mitya had played his symphony for Walter the winter before in Leningrad, where Walter was guest conductor of the Philharmonic. "I don't remember for sure," says Bruno Walter, "who brought Shostakovich to see me. I think it was Nikolai Malko." The conductor and the young composer met in the empty hall of the Philharmonic; they could not converse much, for Mitya spoke no German and Walter no Russian, but Walter was impressed by the earnestness that shone from the thoughtful eyes behind their heavy horn-rimmed glasses. Mitya played his symphony on the piano while Walter followed the score. The conductor was "struck at once by this magnificent work, by its true symphonic form," and immediately promised to present it in Berlin.

Walter kept his promise and Dmitri went to the German capital and sat unnoticed in the packed hall, listening to the audience cheer his music. "I did not even know Shostakovich was in Berlin," relates Walter, "until two nights later when he rang the bell of my apartment at eleven thirty. It was an unusual hour for callers in Berlin, but apparently not for a Russian."

Bruno Walter was the first to play Mitya's music in western Europe. During the following years he presented the First Symphony several times, both in Vienna and in Munich.

When Mitya returned to Leningrad, his sister Marusia observed that he had brought home with him a few Western touches. He had suddenly begun to pay minute attention to the neatness of his coat, and the youthful bangs above his horn-rimmed glasses had been combed to the side.

Just after he came home, on Easter night, Mitya had

an attack of appendicitis. He was taken to the hospital the next day and the operation was performed by Petrashevskaya, assistant to their old friend Dr. Grekov, who was ill himself. The operation was successful and the family hoped it would have no bad effects on Mitya's tuberculosis. Marusia wrote: "He has been put in a separate room and the first two nights after the operation Mother spent with him. But now she is allowed there only in the daytime and comes home at night."

It was while Mitya was convalescing that he met a young girl by the name of Nina Varzar. She was a student of physics at the Polytechnical Institute. Nina, or Nita as she was called at home, was the youngest of three daughters in the Varzar family; they lived in a luxurious apartment in the best section of Leningrad along the banks of the Neva River. The unusual name of Varzar was derived from the father's Bulgarian or Moldavian ancestry. The three sisters, Elena, Ludmilla, and Nina, were not great beauties, but they dressed always in a worldly and pleasing manner. The two older sisters were artistically endowed; Elena (or Nelly) was a painter and was married to a cartoonist, and Ludmilla was an architect. It was after her designs that one of the workers' commissaries was built in Moscow. Their house was always full of artists and the atmosphere was one of sophisticated bohemianism. Nina was the quietest of the three and her interests lay only in her academic studies.

For the first time Mitya forgot the shyness and awkwardness that his cousin Tanya had accused him of; he began to see a great deal of young Nina, with her blond hair and brown eyes.

But the young romantic was not distracted at all from his work, and that spring he embarked on a most important task. "Once my studies were finished," he relates, "it became necessary for me to overhaul a great part of the musical baggage that I had acquired. I understood that music was not only a combination of sounds disposed in this or that order, but an art capable of expressing, by the proper means, the most diverse ideas or sentiments. This conviction I did not acquire without pain. It suffices to say that during the year 1926 I did not write a single note, but from 1927 on I have never ceased to compose." [7]

In the spring of 1927 he was commissioned by the government to write a symphony commemorating the tenth anniversary of the October Revolution (so called because the Soviet Revolution took place in the month of October according to the old-style Russian calendar). He was to write music that would celebrate the achievements of a great revolution, the achievements of the proletariat — to write "proletarian music," as it was later designated. And so young Dmitri Shostakovich became a Soviet Composer.

---

[7] *La Revue Musicale*, December 1936.

Chapter 7.

THE RUSSIAN of today may explain that, though the term "Soviet Composer" is still used with reference to all modern Russian composers whose art was born since the Revolution — and therefore serves to distinguish them from the old Russian composers — the name "proletarian composer" or "proletarian music" belongs to the early days of the Revolution and is now hardly necessary.[1] The first part of the statement is partly true; the second part is not true at all. The word "proletarian" still exists, and words equivalent to it or even more complicated, such as "Socialistic Thematic" — all meaning the same thing. And it will exist as long as the masses are referred to as the proletariat. If it is not heard as often now, it is because the Western ear is antagonized by it and its association with the word "masses," which suggests to the Western mind the word "mob."

---

[1] The term "proletarian" as used here has no connection with the organization known as "Russian Association of Proletarian Musicians," which existed from 1924 to 1932.

The whole question of these terms is not too simple a matter, for it involves more than merely a means of identification. The Westerner will find himself on very slippery ground as long as he persists in trying to fit the meaning of the term "proletarian" to his own standards, or to think of it on the order of "Of the proletarian, by the proletarian, and for the proletarian." Soviet music does not have to be *of* the proletarian; music with a proletarian subject, although most welcome, is not imperative. It may be composed *by* a proletarian, but it does not have to be and in most cases is not. But it must be written *for* the proletarian — that is, written in the musical medium that will reach the masses and not the select few.

The men who were building a new society in Soviet Russia, based on new moral and economic foundations, had also to find a place in this new life for art — that human activity which absorbs more forces than any other in society except the military. Russian intellect has always been very strongly influenced by Leo Tolstoy, and, as one finds in Tolstoy's works a great many wise utterances about art now attributed to Lenin, it is reasonable to presume that Tolstoy's *What is Art?* lay at the foundations of the new æsthetic ideas.

Every great philosopher since the time of Aristotle and Plato had dealt with the problem of æsthetics in human society; among these giants the Russians found one of their own race, Leo Tolstoy, who spoke to them directly of the needs of their own society — who spoke to them in their own language. And Tolstoy spoke Russian very well.

What is Art? is a collection of essays written in 1897. There is a great deal in these essays that cannot be flatly accepted, even under such an august name as Tolstoy's; certain strong prejudices regarding famous poets, musicians, writers, and painters must be discarded as utter rubbish, unworthy of the author. But there are pages that could be used as they stand as a foundation for a constitution of art in Soviet Russia, were such a one to be written.

On art, says Tolstoy, as on war, human lives are wasted outright. Thousands of men devote their entire lives to perfecting themselves in their particular art.

And such people [writes Tolstoy], who frequently are very good, clever men, capable of any useful work, grow wild in these exclusive, stupefying occupations and become dulled to all serious phenomena of life — one-sided and completely self-complacent specialists, who know only how to twirl their legs, their tongues, or their fingers. . . .

It would be well if the artists did all their work themselves, but as it is, they need the aid of workmen, not only for the production of the art, but also for their usually luxurious maintenance, and in one way or another they receive it, either in the form of pay from rich people, or through subsidies from the government, which are given them by the millions for theaters, conservatories, academies. This money is collected from the masses, some of whom have to sell their cow to pay the taxes and who never enjoy these æsthetic pleasures which art gives.

It was all very well for the Greek or the Roman artist, or even for our artists of the first half of our century (when there were slaves and it was considered right that there should be), with a calm conscience to make men serve him and his pleasure; but in our time, when in all men there is at least some dim perception of the equality of men, it is impossible to make people work for art against their will, without having first decided the question whether it is true that art is so good and important an affair that it redeems this evil.

If not, it is terrible to consider that it may very easily happen that terrific sacrifices in labor, in human life, in morality, are made for art's sake, while that same art may be not only useless, but even harmful.

And so for a society amidst which the productions of art arise and are supported, it is necessary to know whether all is really art which professes to be such, and whether all that is art is good, as it is considered to be in our society, and whether, if it is good, it is important and deserves all these sacrifices which are demanded in its name.

To think that proletarian music must be on a relatively low æsthetic level is to disregard the taste of the proletariat, who should be the sole judge of it.

The assertion that art [writes Tolstoy] may be good art and yet be incomprehensible to a great majority of men is to such a degree incorrect, its consequences are to such a degree pernicious for art . . . that it is impossible to make sufficiently clear its whole absurdity.

We have become accustomed to such an assertion, and yet to say that a work of art is good but not comprehensible is the same as to say of a certain food that it is very good but that men cannot eat it. . . . Corrupted art may be comprehensible to men, but good art is always comprehensible to all men. . . . As men may habituate themselves to decayed food, to whisky, tobacco, or opium, so they can habituate themselves to bad art, as is actually being done.

Moreover, we cannot say that the majority of men have no taste for the appreciation of the highest productions of art.

The obstacle to the understanding of the highest, the best sentiments (as it says in the Gospel) lies by no means in a lack of development and teaching, but, on the contrary, in a false development and a false teaching. A good and lofty work of art may indeed be incomprehensible to the erudite and perverted, but not to simple, uncorrupted working people (to them everything which is very high is comprehensible). . . .

Thus good, great, universal art may be incomprehensible only to a small circle of corrupted men, and not to any large number of plain men.

The reason why art cannot be incomprehensible to the masses is not that it is very good, as the artists of our time are fond of saying. It would be more correct to suppose that art is incomprehensible to the great masses only because this art is very bad or even no art at all.

They say: "Works of art are not liked by the people, because they are incapable of understanding them." But if the works of art have for their aim the infection of men with the emotion which the artist experienced, how can we speak of lack of comprehension?

Mussorgsky, whom Dmitri considered the greatest of the Russian composers, expressed this dominant idea of bringing music into closer relationship with actual life, in a letter to Stassov: "To seek assiduously the most delicate and subtle features of human nature — of the human crowd — to follow them into unknown regions, to make them our own . . . this seems to me the true vocation of the artist . . . to feed upon humanity as a healthy diet which has been neglected — there lies the whole problem of art." Mussorgsky, like Dmitri, was the product of a period of moral and intellectual ferment; the new artistic doctrine that swept the country after the emancipation of the serfs was "Hold out the hand of fellowship to the liberated masses and learn from them the true purpose of life."

Dmitri himself has said: "I consider that every artist who isolates himself from the world is doomed. I find it incredible that an artist should want to shut himself away from the people, who, in the end, form his audience. I think an artist should serve the greatest possible number of people. I always try to make myself as widely understood as possible, and, if I don't succeed, I consider it my own fault." [2]

The musical literature of the Soviet Union forms only another item in the immense wealth of its citizens and, as such, cannot be enjoyed by the select few. By this same token, artistic media must be used that will appeal to the greatest number. Just as futurism and cubism and even impressionism in painting are not

_____
[2] *New York Times,* December 20, 1931.

greatly favored in the Soviet Union, so atonal music, or music full of mysticism, remains alien to the Soviet idea.

Shostakovich says of Scriabin, at one time a leading Russian composer: "Thus we regard Scriabin as our bitterest musical enemy. Why? Because Scriabin's music tends to an unhealthy eroticism. Also to mysticism and passivity and escape from the realities of life."

Beethoven was immediately adopted by the Soviets. Stories of Beethoven as a revolutionary fit neatly into the Soviet idea. There is the well-known story of his Third Symphony, the Eroica. Beethoven dedicated it to Napoleon when he thought Napoleon was a revolutionist. When Napoleon became Emperor, Beethoven tore up the dedication page. There is also the less well-known story of Beethoven and Goethe. The two were walking together at one of the Austrian watering-places when, in the course of their stroll along the promenade, they came face to face with the Austrian King and Queen. Goethe, the courtier by birth and breeding, swept off his hat in a low bow. Beethoven jerked down the brim of his, clapped his hands behind his back, and strode on. Later Goethe reproached him for his rudeness to royalty. Beethoven replied: "You, Goethe, can create any amount of kings and queens. But no king or queen has ever created a Goethe."

Lenin, whose every word and reaction was held in awe, was by no means a lover of music. Like so many Russian intellectuals he felt that music should be followed immediately by the action it inspires. "We must not stay here any longer," he said once to Maxim Gorky, as he led him away from the concert they were attending; "this music makes one soft."

This point of view belongs more to the Russians than to any other race. It is strongly expressed by Leo Tolstoy in *The Kreutzer Sonata*. His character Pozdnis-chev says: "It is a different thing if a military march is played; then the soldiers move forward, keeping time to the music, and the end is attained. If dance music is played, people dance to it, and the object is also accomplished; if a mass is sung, I receive Holy Communion, and here, too, the music is not in vain. But take the Kreutzer Sonata for example: is it right to play that first presto in a drawing-room to the ladies in low-cut dresses?"

Lenin, however, it is reported on reliable authority, once heard Issay Dobrowen, conductor and pianist, play Beethoven's Appassionata Sonata and liked it very much. Though this was by no means the signal for clasping Beethoven to the bosom of Soviet music, it was a helpful benediction and added to the weight of Beethoven's popularity.

Just as Beethoven was hailed throughout the country as an example of a revolutionary composer, many others, and notably Russians, were banned. This has always been the case with the promulgation of a new idea. Tolstoy speaks of it with relation to religion: "Always, at all times and in every human society, there exists a religious sense, common to all men of this society, of what is good and what bad, and this religious conception decides the worth of the sentiments conveyed by art. And so with all nations the art which conveys sentiments arising from the religious sense common to the men of that nation has been recognized as good and has been encouraged; but the art which conveys feelings which do not agree with this religious consciousness has been considered bad and has been rejected; all the remaining immense field of art, by means of which men communicate one with another, has not been at all appreciated and has been noticed only when it ran counter to the religious conception of its age. Thus it was with all the nations — with the Greeks, the Jews, the Hindus, the Egyptians, the Chinese; and thus it was at the appearance of Christianity."

In the young Soviet Republic the works of Tchaikovsky, Glinka, and others, whose music or operatic plots reminded the listeners of czarism and the old regime, were out — their names did not appear on programs until 1932 and 1933. By then the Soviets felt themselves so sure in the saddle that they considered their audiences well prepared to take these works in the right spirit — to accept them for their musical values, and as ancient and outlived history.

The young Soviet composer of today has been thoroughly educated in these ideas, and it would be a mistake to compare him with an American boy who, after good work at a top-ranking music school, will pack up and go to Europe to get a sniff and a scrap of the old culture and come home to settle down and write music as freely as a bird sings. It is not necessary to emphasize the fact that innumerable gems of the world's music literature are the product of just such a "careless rapture"; but under the new Soviet æsthetics no such Schubertian frivolity could be tolerated as its foundation.

"There can be no music without ideology," said Shostakovich in an interview with a correspondent of the *New York Times*. "The old composers, whether they knew it or not, were upholding a political theory. Most of them of course were bolstering the rule of the upper classes. Only Beethoven was a forerunner of the revolutionary movement. If you will read his letters you will see how often he wrote his friends that he wished to give new ideas to the public and rouse it to revolt against its masters. On the other hand, Wagner's biographies show that he began his career as a radical and ended as a reactionary. His monarchistic patriotism had a bad effect on his mind. . . . We, as revolutionists, have a different conception of music. Lenin himself said that 'music is a means of unifying broad masses of people.' [8] It is not a leader of masses, perhaps, but certainly an organizing force. . . . Even the symphonic form, which appears more than any other to be divorced from literary elements, can be said to

---

[8] This idea Lenin takes directly from Tolstoy's *What is Art?*

have a bearing on politics. . . . Music is no longer an end in itself, but a vital weapon in the struggle. Because of this, Soviet music will probably develop along different lines from any the world has ever known."

It is in this service that Soviet composers are engaged, and, as such, belong completely, body and soul, to that one vast organization, of which music is only a part, that serves the proletariat. The Soviet composer enjoys privileges and an esteem in the Soviet Union far greater than artists in any other society, but his bondage and his duties to the interests of the Soviet Union are airtight. As a citizen of the Soviet Union, he belongs to the proletariat, and his life and his work must serve, in whatever form they express themselves, the people of the Union.

O N the 6th of November 1927 Dmitri's Second Symphony was performed by the Leningrad Philharmonic, at a concert celebrating the tenth anniversary of the Bolshevik Revolution. It was given often throughout that year and at one time was performed simultaneously in four cities, Leningrad, Moscow, Kiev, and Kharkov. The title page of the score reads: "Dm. Shostakovich, opus 14, *To October*, a Symphonic Dedication, with a Closing Chorus written to the words of A. Bezimensky, for Large Orchestra and Mixed Chorus." In the top right-hand corner of the page are the words: "Proletarians of the World, Unite!" This work, in one movement, is, in spite of its stirring dedication, not equal in quality to any part of Dmitri's First Symphony. Dmitri was at that time influenced by the shortlived fad of "industrial music" and even included a factory whistle in his score, but the piece as a whole is ineffective. In his first attempt at deliberately political music Dmitri seems to have failed, for the "October" Symphony did not have brilliant reviews nor has it been performed much since.

The atmosphere on Nikolaevskaya Street had changed. The young Shostakoviches were no longer children, but mature and adult citizens. The success of Dmitri's First Symphony had already begun to have beneficial results, and in spite of the fact that jealousy still made him enemies, his talent was definitely recognized. For the first time the family's grinding daily worries seemed of less importance and they were able to pay more attention to the life around them.

They had not left Leningrad that summer, for Dmitri had much work to do. Zoya got herself a job with the Geological Committee, her character improved, and she acquired a sudden maturity. Marusia, after her years of periodic "flirtations" and broken hearts, had finally fallen in love.

Vsevolod Constantinovich Frederichs was eighteen years her senior. He was a professor of physics at the Polytechnical Institute. Years before, he had been a student at Göttingen at the same time as Nadejda, and the two had been inseparable friends. It was through Nadejda that he met the Shostakovich family, and Marusia had known him since her childhood. She had always liked him and in her adolescent days had made of him her "father confessor" for all of her youthful love affairs. But nothing made him so popular with her as his admiration of and devotion to Nadejda, whom Marusia loved. She married him in the fall of 1927, and on a postcard to Nadejda she quoted Vsevolod as saying that years ago in Göttingen he used to tell Nadejda that he was going to marry Marusia, who was then only seven.

As Marusia was leaving the Nikolaevskaya Street house, Mitya said to her: "Don't come home for at least a year." Whatever happened, he thought she should give it one year's fair trial.

Now Marusia was busier than ever — with her new home and her lessons. She still held her job at the ballet school; her piano lessons she continued to give on Nikolaevskaya Street, for there was no piano in her own house. Two friends of the family moved into Marusia's old room. A short time afterwards a son of theirs married suddenly. Marusia wrote: "Just imagine — little Boris suddenly got married. He is not earning anything and now he brings a wife to his parents to support. Mother and I were thinking what would happen if Mitya came and announced that *he* was getting married!"

Two years later, in the spring of 1929, Dmitri did, in fact, make this announcement. He was going to marry Nina Varzar. Marusia, who by this time had a little son, Mitya, had come to see Sonya one afternoon and her mother told her the news. Despite the shock that they all felt, both girls and Sonya wanted to be as sweet and diplomatic as possible in handling the situation. They sent a box of flowers to Nina and that evening they called on the Varzar family, "with the best

Zoya at twenty-one.

Marusia at the age of twenty-seven.

and the sweetest intentions," as Marusia put it. But they were met with a cold reception. The bride-to-be never appeared and they were "not even offered a cup of tea." Nina's mother announced that she had already found the place for Dmitri and Nina to live — in Detskoye Selo. Sonya, taken aback, reminded her that Mitya still had a mother and a sister. But Mme Varzar remarked that of course Sonya could not expect to live with them. "Mother grew gray and then red — and I took her home."

They were very upset and Marusia described their visit to Dmitri; but Sonya neither said nor did anything to interfere with her son's intentions. She congratulated him, bought champagne, and went out of her way to be pleasant to Nina; but she sometimes wept by herself.

Leningrad buzzed with rumors — Shostakovich was getting married, but his future mother-in-law wouldn't have Sonya live with her son any longer; he would perish in that atmosphere. It was said that Shostakovich's mother was given ten days to leave her son's apartment. Sonya bore this talk quietly and told Dmitri that she was ready to leave any time he wished her to; she was not, after all these years, afraid of hardship.

Dmitri's nerves were badly upset by the situation and he was near a breakdown. He entered a sanatorium and sent formal word to Nina that the marriage was off. Sonya wrote that she was convinced that this decision was in no way influenced by her, that Dmitri had given her his word of honor that this was so, and that for the last three years he had been completely independent of her. She added that he was always surrounded by a great many friends who had more influence on him than an old mother. She thought Dmitri must have realized that this was no time for a boy of twenty-two, whose career had only begun, who needed all his freedom for his work, and whose financial state was not yet too secure, to burden himself with a marriage. He was swamped with work that was not completed and his brilliant career would make more and more demands on his time and energy.

*   *   *

Ivan Sollertinsky, a Leningrad music-critic and one of the most brilliant musicologists in Russia, who was later to become Dmitri's inseparable friend, writes: "As a creative character, Shostakovich is far removed from the romantic ideal of an artist who works only when he is inspired, possessed, or plunged into a state of divine folly. Above all, he is a professional who has the command of the technique in any genre. He is even inclined to emphasize the artisan quality of the musical profession. He works a great deal and writes rapidly, often without rough drafts. He composes in full score, without preliminary sketches for piano. Like a trained chess-player who can play simultaneous games on several chess-boards, Shostakovich can work on several musical compositions, at times on contrasting psychological planes."

While Dmitri was writing his Second Symphony, he was already planning his first opera, based on Gogol's story *The Nose*. In an article that was later printed with the libretto and entitled "Why *The Nose?*" he writes:

I planned the opera in the summer of 1928. I had to turn to Gogol for the subject for the following reasons: The Soviet writers have produced a great many important works, but for me, who am not a professional author, it was very hard to work them into an opera libretto. The authors of these works did not come to meet me half-way in this respect, giving as a reason either that they had no time to spare from their own work, or (here I may be mistaken, in which case I should like the authors whom I approached to answer) on account of insufficient interest in the development of Soviet opera art. I was forced to turn to the classics. Considering that in our time an opera based on a classical subject would be pertinent —·providing it has a satirical character — I began to look for this subject in the works of the three titans of Russian satire: Gogol, Saltykov-Shchedrin, and Chekhov. Finally I chose Gogol's *The Nose*. Why *The Nose* out of all of Gogol's works?

It is sufficient to read the story to be convinced that *The Nose*, as a satire on the epoch of Nicholas I, is stronger than any other story of Gogol's. Furthermore, it seemed to me that this story would be easier for me to make into an opera than *Dead Souls*. I repeat that the short literary form is easier for me to adapt to the stage than the long. And, finally, the text of *The Nose* is more sparkling in its language and more expressive than any other among Gogol's "Petersburg Tales"; it presents many interesting problems in putting it into music, as well as many interesting dramatic situations.

About the libretto: The libretto is composed on a literary pattern. The changes from Gogol's original story are as follows: The scene which Gogol has in the market-

Dmitri at the time of his opera, " The Nose."
From a drawing by N. Radlov.

place is transposed to the Kazansky Cathedral (the scene in the Kazansky Cathedral was forbidden by the censorship of Nicholas I, and Gogol was forced to put it in the market-place). The scene of catching the nose is far more fully developed than in Gogol, who only indicates it.

About the music: The music in this production is not predominant; the text is the more important. I wish to add that the music does not deliberately have the character of parody. No! In spite of the humor on the stage, the music is not comical. I consider this correct, because Gogol relates all the comedy situations in a serious manner. In this lies the remarkable force of Gogol's humor. Gogol never "wisecracks" — and the music does not try to do so either.

The opera was produced on the 18th of January 1930, in the Mikhailovsky Theater. It had a sound success, but was considered technically very difficult and has not been done often since.

Reviewing the opera, the well-known critic and writer Victor M. Belayev, said: "As one makes the acquaintance of the new opera by Shostakovich, one is apt, unintentionally, to compare it to Mussorgsky's *Matchmaker* and Dargomijsky's *Stone Guest*. This comparison is not to the detriment but in favor of Shostakovich's opera." Shostakovich solved a problem which had interested Russian composers for a long time — the problem of "opera dialogue" — and Belayev finds in *The Nose* what he considers "the musical equivalent of a great literary work." In the three works mentioned above he sees a trend toward creating a musical speech which would be speech and music at the same time. Alban Berg had been working on this musical and artistic problem, which originated with Russian composers, and achieved a great deal in this respect in his opera *Wozzek*. It is therefore not surprising that there is a resemblance to Berg's *Wozzek* in the treatment of the vocal parts of *The Nose*.

The turn of our everyday speech is developed by us in our communication with those around us and the same process works with the cultivation of the musical language of the composer. He, too, learns a great deal from his "elders," from composers who have already found their own language and who have fixed its peculiarities in their compositions. There is evidence in *The Nose* of much that Dmitri learned from Berg, and besides Berg from Prokofiev and Stravinsky. All this influence, however, does not detract from the young Shostakovich's personal traits, any more than did the influence of Glinka on the music of Dargomijsky and of Wagner on the music of Rimsky-Korsakov. It serves merely to bring out vividly the young composer's individuality and to show the direction of his artistic tendencies. As Goethe once said: "If I could give an account of all that I owe to great predecessors and contemporaries, there would be but a small balance in my favor."

Speaking of the opera itself, Belayev wrote that, despite its great artistic qualities, it presented quite a problem to produce. "The chamber-music style in which it is written and the extremely difficult mode of musical declamation which is used in treating the vocal parts manifest the development of a new style in our music for which we have not, as yet, the performers. This, of course, does not mean that we shall not have such performers. It means only that we shall have to develop them if we want such operas as Shostakovich's *The Nose* to be given the performances the opera deserves — meaning excellent."

During the year he was working on the opera, life was very full for Dmitri; the apartment on Nikolaevskaya Street became a popular meeting-place for poets, musicians, and artists. During this time Dmitri made an orchestral transcription for woodwind ensemble of two pieces by Scarlatti, composed ten pieces for piano which he called *Aphorisms*, a Sonata for piano, and music for the film *New Babylon*.[1]

Dmitri, when he was not in Leningrad, was in Moscow writing music for Meyerhold's theater. It was there that he wrote the incidental music for Mayakovsky's comedy *The Bedbug*.[2] He was well paid for this work, but he did not enjoy it and was always drawn back to Leningrad; and although his family was glad to have him back, they knew that it meant much less money coming in. Dmitri did not bring much cheer into the house these days; he was tired and unhappy and spoke

---

[1] Of these, only the Sonata, a rather immature work, is known in this country. The music for *New Babylon* remains in manuscript, and the Scarlatti transcriptions, which were also in manuscript, have been lost.

[2] This music remains in manuscript.

seldom, and then abruptly. They knew the reason for it, but were powerless to help him.

Sonya had been without a job for a long time and she resigned herself to taking care of the house. She did the marketing, the house-cleaning, and the cooking and twice a week at night she did the washing. She was tired and ill, but she had a new source of happiness these days that gave her strength: she was a grand-mother. She wrote to Nadejda that this new feeling made her forget everything. She said that she had never before felt such love for a child — not even for her own — as she felt for Marusia's baby, Mitya. "As I work at home, the charming little face, with gray-blue eyes, of the gay plump baby stands before my eyes and I am in a hurry to do what I have to do at home so that I can go to Marusia and fuss over my grandson."

She was at Marusia's every day for she felt that she should help Marusia, who had her job and so many lessons to give besides. She often spent her nights there, for when everything was quiet and everybody had gone to sleep she could be alone with the baby. Little Mitya slept well, and Sonya sat beside his bed night after night contentedly watching him and letting her thoughts drift slowly through her head.

Our baby is such a darling and it is such happiness for me to feel him so close to me. Even my weariness flies away somewhere and I could spend hours sitting and look-ing at him. In the quiet of the night old memories and old faces go by in procession. . . . My futile and unhappy life passes before me, with all its sorrows and mistakes of the last years. Sometimes dear images appear in my memory, little unimportant events, for some reason, out of the early days of my youth — life in the institute, the years in the first cozy little house in the gold fields, the garden, the fountain, and the Bodaybo bridge. And then the years with Dmitri Boleslavovich — how I would have laughed if someone had predicted my life two months before Dmitri died . . . all those seven years of work with never a day off . . . all the humiliation and suffering I went through! All for what? It was I who fell in everybody's eyes, I am the only one who is at fault. It will be hard to believe that I am to blame for spoiling every friendship and every relation in our family. . . . And you, my little Zoyusha — there is no greater grief for me than when you sometimes slam out of the house. My dear little girl, I am sorry that I cannot help you — from the constant insults and sorrow I have become a frightened and pitiful creature — but, believe me, you all still need me and only this binds me to life. I beg you to be generous and kind, for how many times I want to talk with you more than anyone! But you are always against me — always, right from my first words, begin to suspect me of something, and I, from cowardice, say what I shouldn't. Believe me, I suffer terribly — I never wake up happy and I never really sleep. All my life in the last years has been one long suffering. . . . Believe me, my little girl, I am ill and tired, and when a human being is so sick, the head doesn't work properly — it becomes empty. Please understand me and don't condemn me. . . . Could anyone believe those years of struggle, when I was taking care of my children and saving them from hunger and cold — and naïvely thought that everyone should help me? Now, when the desperate struggle is far behind me, it is especially painful to think of those whom I have hurt . . . I know that tomorrow is assured for my children, but I cannot become resigned to the thought that I have lost the friendship and the faith of my dearest friends and of my family. . . . How could I think of "equality," when there is born into a family a creation like my son Mitya? Where can the question of equality enter? With whom could one compare him? How pale and colorless are all his cousins and their friends. . . . Vera's children are all so healthy and earn so much — but what are their interests — repeating all the stories of our lives in Bodaybo, of our youth — who cares — what of it? Vera brings them up with small personal interests, when the life around them beats with such a tempo! I consider that every citizen in our country should take part in building the new life and should be proud of what he is doing. In those years of struggle I learned to love work and modest living. . . . Suppose, for instance, the ceiling of our house fell in — whom should one save? Of course Mitya — for this would be the duty of everyone to society, for the sake of art — disregarding all personal feeling. . . . And now Mitya is unhappy and we cannot help him. I work at home all I can, but the years are telling on me — I need a rest, a cure. I have rheumatism in my arms and legs and such a cold pain in my arms all the way from the shoulder . . . I still wear my thin coat and the shoes that are too heavy for my aching feet. . . . Marusia is taken care of, but her husband doesn't like me any more — nor, I guess, does Marusia either. I am only a "poor old relative" who can nurse the baby, and I am happy to serve. The other day I brought a little Angora kitten just to amuse the baby. I carried it all the way from Nikolaevskaya Street — I was

not allowed on the street-car with it and so I walked. But
they wouldn't let me leave the kitten here with the baby
— not even for one day. I carried him all the way back —
my legs were tired and my hands hurt — it was dark and
the kitten kept jumping out of my hands and I cried. . . .
Tomorrow morning, I will run home early so that I can fix
tea and get fresh rolls for Mitya and Zoya before they
wake up. . . . It always seems to me the street-cars are
crawling and I wish I had magic feet. . . .

*   *   *

Dmitri's Third Symphony — the "May First" Symphony, dedicated to the international labor holiday —
had its premiere in Leningrad on November 6, 1930.
This work, like the "October" Symphony, is in one
movement, with a choral ending. The text of the
chorus is in the nature of a call to revolutionary uprising throughout the world, and the rhythm is that of a
marching song. This symphony was described by its
composer as a "proletarian tract in tones."

Dmitri was now definitely established as a composer;
his works were being played in foreign countries and
his fame was spreading. He traveled throughout Russia
in connection with his work, and had made his first air-
plane trip. He went to the Caucasus for a rest whenever
he had a breathing-space. He seemed to have money
for everything he needed; but Sonya was over-sensitive
about his supporting the family entirely and she did
all the hard work in the house in order to justify her
living there.

Marusia's happiness seemed to be complete. She admired and loved her husband; she was the sister of a brilliant musician whose fame had even reached America, and the mother of a fine little boy. They lived in a spacious apartment that was supplied to Frederichs by the university, and with her husband's earnings and her own increased salary at the school she could afford practically all she wanted.

As for Zoya, once again as so often before, she was left out. Sonya would not allow Zoya to take any money from her brother, all the help that came from America was still going to Jasha's family, and Marusia, probably owing to the rigorous sacrifices she had had to make during the hard years, now held on to everything she had and shared nothing with her younger sister. Zoya still worked and contributed her share to the household, and her only pleasure was the keen interest in sports which she had recently acquired. Her interest may have been partly due to the fact that, in sports, clothes were of less importance than the natural youthful beauty of which she had a great deal, and partly because sports gave her a release for her superabundance of dare-devil energy.

In the summer of 1931 Zoya went away from home for the first time; she spent that vacation by herself in the Caucasus. Here in a small resort she saw again a handsome young man whom she had met once before in Moscow — Gregory Constantinovich Kruschchov, professor of histology at the University of Moscow. At the end of two months they were engaged. Zoya returned to Leningrad, and on the 22nd of September Gregory Constantinovich came up from Moscow.

He made a most favorable impression on both the Frederichs and the Shostakovich family. Sonya gave them a dinner party with a few relatives present. They were all amused at how Zoya, the *"enfant terrible,"* had suddenly been changed and mellowed by love. In the afternoon, after dinner, Dmitri performed the last act from his opera *The Nose* to his own piano accompaniment. This was a wedding-present for Zoya.

"Just as Mitya told me," wrote Marusia later, "when I married Vsevolod: 'Don't return home before the year is up,' so we said the same thing to Zoya. Now we shall see how long she will live outside of our home. With me it was different, because I live in the same city and can see the family every day — but you can't ride up and down all the time from Moscow and, besides, her job in Moscow won't let her get away. Right now she writes us very happy letters, and we are very glad that he is older than she is. We are so accustomed to looking on her as a giddy little girl."

As Sonya put it, her family nest was falling apart; she was left alone with Dmitri. "To live with Mitya is the greatest happiness, to be close to his magnetic personality."

But Dmitri had been working unusually hard this year and he left for the Caucasus for a brief rest very soon afterwards. He had written a great deal of incidental music for the moving pictures, had done much work in connection with the newly developed talking films, his two ballets, *The Bolt* and *The Golden Age*, were in performance, and he had had to attend rehearsals and meetings.

At about this time, he was interviewed by a correspondent of the *New York Times*, who came to the apartment on Nikolaevskaya Street, where "there was a pair of angora kittens romping on the floor" and "in the background was a gentle, gray-haired mother. . . ." In the course of the interview Dmitri confessed, with "some embarrassment," that he was writing a new opera, and he added that it was a secret. "Apparently it would be a lengthy and ambitious affair," writes the correspondent. " 'I am afraid I may never finish it,' said he. 'But you have finished other important things.' 'I don't know, I don't know.' He shook his head unhappily, quite ignoring his past record of accomplishment." [3]

Dmitri meant his opera *Lady Macbeth of the Mzensk District*, the first part of a great tetralogy that was to be one of his most important achievements.

His work and his successes did little, however, to lift his low spirits. "I was born under an unlucky star," he used to say to his mother, and both she and his adoring sister would console themselves with the thought that

---

[3] Interview by Rose Lee, December 1931; quoted by courtesy of the *New York Times*.

all great people were unhappy — though in Dmitri's case they knew well what was troubling his heart, but didn't dare to mention it. Sonya adapted herself to her son's every mood; she cared for him and managed the house, never disturbed him at his work, never told him of all that was in her heart. Her greatest joy was to go to all the performances of Dmitri's music, and no sooner were they announced than she would buy herself a ticket. She loved *The Nose* and never missed a performance. She thought that the "Dance of the Red Army" in the ballet *The Bolt* was magnificent, and that the organ fugue in his music for the *Golden Mountains* was fantastic and wonderful — the music for this film she considered his best work so far. This revolutionary picture, with music by her son, stirred Sonya far more than had any of the actual scenes of the revolution that she must have seen so often.

In the summer of 1932 Sonya received a letter from Omsk announcing the death of her older sister, Vera. "I took this news rather calmly," she wrote, "feeling more a quiet grief than shock. For my turn is not 'far beyond the mountains.' Vera died just like Father — she just went to sleep. . . ."

Sonya was sorry that she hadn't managed to go to see her sister, but she had other news that was far closer to her. "We have an event at home that will no doubt change my life radically," she wrote. "My Mityusha suddenly married without saying one word to me." Dmitri had married Nina Varzar on the 13th of May,

and the bride come to live in the apartment on Nikolaevskaya Street.

You have been too long away, my dear Aunt Nadia
[wrote Marusia], and cannot imagine what a home we
had on Nikolaevskaya Street. One couldn't find another
such home — though we didn't have any luxury, or an
attractive exterior, the air there was different — and this
not only *we* say, but also our friends. And now everything
is finished here — it is a veritable graveyard. I feel I cannot
tell you properly what has happened — but what composed and made up our happiness has ended. What was
there — certainly created by Mother — I could not dupli-
cate in my own family even if I tried to imitate it. Zoya
has not been away from home long enough — what will
happen with her home is hard to predict now. . . .
Vsevolod Constantinovich always said that one should
not spoil a boy the way we did Mitya. Perhaps he is right,
but after all it was Mother who created and nourished his
talent. It was so hard for us, Aunt Nadia, after Father's
death — so very hard. Mother could have let Mitya become a cabaret player — she could have let him go on
playing in the movies, where he could eventually have
made a lot of money and we could have lived very well.
But Mother understood that this would have killed him
and she tried in every way and succeeded in creating for
him the conditions necessary for his work and his talent.
. . . Our greatest fault is that we worshipped him, all
three of us. But I don't regret it. For, after all, he is a really
great man now. Frankly speaking, he has a very difficult
character — he is rough with us, hardly speaks to us, and
at the same time he is terribly attached to Mother. Toward
those close to him his character is just impossible. . . .

But the most terrible of all is that there is no longer our good Shostakovich family. Zoya and I — Mamma tells us we two must hold on to each other and that the life that we had on Nikolaevskaya Street and everything that is bound with that apartment should be the brightest spot in our life. . . .

Zoya is here right now; she arrived a few days ago and is living with Mother and Mitya. She is expecting a baby from day to day. I hope she will have a girl — a bad daughter is better than a good son. A daughter will always stay with her mother but a son will leave and behave like a fool. . . . My child is a darling boy, but probably in twenty years he will bring his mother the same kind of surprise as Mitya did. . . . Please, darling Nadia, write to Mother very sweetly — it is so hard for her now. She is so tired from all this, and now she is worried about Zoya. When you receive this letter, we shall have a boy — or a girl. The date was supposed to have been yesterday; Zoya had a pain in her back and spasms. Mother and I took her to the hospital, but the doctor says it is nothing of the kind — it still may be another three weeks. Zoika is furious — she is so tired of waiting.

In Sonya's first letter after Dmitri's marriage she expressed herself as resigned to it. She was chiefly concerned about what would happen to his creative progress, and this stage of it had ended so banally. This, she admitted, was great egotism on her part, since he loved his wife and found great happiness with her. Well then, she thought, so be it.

Right now we are all living together — but I shall have to arrange my life separately, I don't know yet how. Perhaps I will stay here and they will move to a new apartment — the directors of the Academic Theaters have promised Mitya a new apartment. Perhaps I will move to Moscow. I am afraid it is going to be hard for me here — farther away it will be easier. "Out of sight, out of mind." How I will live through separation from Mitya I cannot yet imagine. How will I live . . . not waiting for his awakening in the morning, and not opening the door for him when he comes home? Those thoughts I push away. It is my greatest satisfaction and happiness to know that it was through my bringing up that he developed, in spite of the difficult years, into a significant composer. . . . Now with sadness I wander about our apartment — the nest is destroyed. In this apartment he grew up — here were recorded all the important events of his musical career — here have been so many celebrities in spite of our poverty, extremely interesting and talented people who visited us constantly. I am so sorry I did not write all that down, but I never had a minute free — nor do I now. From morning till night, winter and summer, I am always at work. Still I hope that everything will be for the best for Mitya — and as for me, I have not long to live. . . . We are modest people, we love work and a modest life. We despise luxury and gluttony. I consider Marusia and Zoya heroic women . . . and yet with most people it is something different — money, money, money. How will Mityusha stand up under all this — big parties, automobiles, expensive restaurants, and so on? It is all so trivial and banal. . . .

I should like to live far away from all of this — I hope that Mitya will be able to help me, but if not I have trained myself in those sixteen years to physical work and I love it. I am not afraid of any kind of job, and I consider work the best remedy for all the ills. I could work in a nursery or in a hospital. . . .

But Nina and Dmitri found that it was impossible to get another apartment in Leningrad that winter, and so they remained in Nikolaevskaya Street and Sonya slept on a couch in the sitting-room, through which everyone had to pass going or coming, and which she never could call her own. She had to fit in somehow with her son's new life and so once again she braced herself to face a difficult task.

*   *   *

On the 23rd of June 1932 Zoya gave birth to a little boy. He was called Nikolai after the street in which the Shostakovich family had lived since 1902. In 1924 the name of the street had been changed to the Street of Marat, for the French revolutionist, but to the Shostakoviches it always remained Nikolaevskaya.

Dmitri and his wife went to the Crimea for the summer, and Sonya moved with Zoya, her husband, and the baby to Peterhof, just outside Leningrad. Here Sonya cooked the meals, managed the house, went into the town marketing, washed the diapers in a near-by brook, fetched water from a well four hundred feet from the house, and carried the heavy slop-jars into the back yard to be emptied. All this she did for the privilege of being with her new grandson and of having a place in her daughter's home.

Once in a while she opened the copy-book in which she had begun to write Dmitri's biography, but she had so little time, she was so discouraged by her lack of literary ability, so generally depressed and tired, that she never went on with it. And yet it was the one thing that she wanted to do now, above all — to "leave something of herself worth while besides the washing of the dishes."

When, in September, it grew cold in the country, they returned to Leningrad. After a short stay there, Zoya and her husband took their baby back to Moscow, and Sonya went back to Nikolaevskaya Street with her son and his wife, where she felt her position had become that of a servant. She knew how easily her work could be taken over by paid help, and she was grateful that she was allowed to stay and do whatever she could. "It is remarkable," wrote Nina Kokaoulin, "how Sonya has adjusted herself to the situation and I admire her for what she is putting up with — all on account of her love for Mitya."

Dmitri had become much quieter. He loved his wife and she loved him — even Sonya could see this. But the difficulties at home, combined with worries about his work, had greatly changed his character; from a gentle happy youngster he had developed into a somber introvert, who was impatient and gruff with those closest to him and hardly spoke to his mother and sister. The conductor Fritz Stiedry, who knew him at that time, describes him as a slender young man with the air of an English aristocrat; the nervous tension that never left him had modeled his face into ascetic lines peculiarly in harmony with his slight frame. Polite and charming, but equally exacting and very stubborn, Dmitri kept himself always withdrawn and aloof, and close intimate contact with him was barred by his reserve.

"I am never happy unless I am up to my ears in work," Dmitri said in an interview with Leonid and Pyotr Tur. "A prolonged rest is a great hardship for me; I find the hardest work is to be away from work. I become sick when I do nothing."

The correspondents continue: "Shostakovich, in the way he works, completely destroys the old myth of the divine powers that guide artists. For him, a musical creation is first of all labor — hard work." What the article goes on to say, in the highly technical terms of the Soviet language, was once stated simply and clearly by Tchaikovsky: "I sit down to the piano regularly at nine o'clock in the morning, and *Mesdames les Muses* have learned to be on time for that rendezvous."

There was only one person outside of his family with whom Dmitri was inseparable, his friend Ivan Sollertinsky, the brilliant young musicologist and ethnologist, the author of many books on Tchaikovsky, Berlioz, Richard Strauss, Schönberg, and others. Sollertinsky held at one time the position of Director of Programs of the Leningrad Philharmonic; he possesses a remarkable memory and an encyclopedic mind, and his exceptional oratorical gifts make him the most popular of the commentators. It was probably due to his influence that Dmitri was so interested in modern European composers like Bruckner, Alban Berg, Hindemith, Schönberg, and Gustav Mahler, particularly the last. The Moscow musicians, true to the tradition of slight jealousy between the two capitals, liked to poke fun at their northern colleague, remarking that "Shostakovich still suffers from Mahleria."

* * *

On New Year's Eve 1932 Sonya sat alone and wrote to her sister Nadejda. Dmitri and Nina had gone to see their friends, Marusia and Vsevolod were celebrating at the university, and Zoya was far away in Moscow. Sonya remembered the days when New Year's Eve was always observed by all of her family together, even during the darkest days of their poverty. But she had resigned herself to what was, and did not think of what should have been. She had suffered greatly, watching the change in her son's character during the past months, and was terrified of upsetting him, lest he leave her behind when he found a new apartment. She implored Nadejda to come to Russia to stay with her, or at least to visit her, she was so alone. Her thoughts drifted, as usual, away from her personal life and turned to the general success in the development of the new life in Russia, of which she was so proud — and then to her son's latest work. "On the 17th of December,

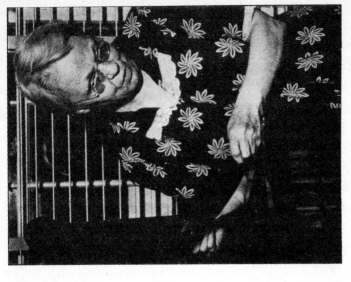

Nadejda listening to one of Dmitri's symphonies.

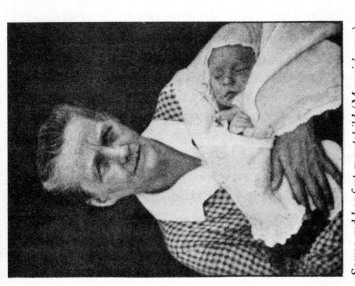

Sonya and her first grandchild (Marusia's son), 1933.

Mitya finished his opera *Lady Macbeth*, and the other day he played it at home for the musical authorities. We all sat spellbound; I should have bought champagne. . . ."

During the spring Dmitri worked on his piano concerto. This concerto is unusually scored — for piano, string orchestra, and trumpet. The trumpet has such an extensive solo part that when Dmitri plays the concerto himself he has the trumpet-player sit down in front at his left and next to the piano. The concerto has four movements, the third being in the nature of a short introduction to the brilliant finale. The general tone of the concerto, except for the lento movement, is one of gay bravado; it sounds as though it might have been written by a schoolboy with his cap set rakishly on the back of his head. Its chief force is in the rhythmic and colorful contrapuntal display; the dissonances, of which Shostakovich is so fond, are not put there merely to shock or startle, but have a definitely logical and organic basis and are inherent in the character of the piece.

The first movement consists of a gay street tune in lively tempo and on what sound to the layman like false notes; it is written with a subtle artistry of counterpoint, giving the impression at first that every man in the orchestra is playing by himself. The second movement seems weak by comparison, for it is simple and Mozartian, on the order of a *valse triste*, but to most hearers it comes as a relief after the fireworks of the first. The short third movement, with a rhapsodic theme in the orchestra, leads to the finale, which is taken at top speed. Gay dance tunes, distinctly Russian in character, form the main subject of this movement, but in the middle of it Shostakovich inserts an ironic parody of the wandering German street bands that play from door to door in Leningrad. The trumpet has the major role here and ample opportunity to display its brilliance in solo and cadenza parts while the rest of the orchestra supports it with deliberately false notes. This is followed by the cadenza for the piano, the only one in the concerto.

This cadenza, the story goes, was written by the composer after he had shown the new concerto to one of his pianist friends. "What — a concerto without a cadenza?" said the annoyed pianist after he had glanced through the pages. "Listen," said Dmitri, "this is not a concerto like one of Tchaikovsky's or Rachmaninoff's, with runs all over the instrument to show you can play scales. This is a bird of a different feather." But his friend's disappointment was so great that Dmitri finally said: "All right, I'll write one." For this cadenza he used the theme from Beethoven's Rondo known as "Rage over a Lost Penny," giving it an ironical treatment of his own. The concerto comes to a breath-taking close with the bugle call of the trumpet sounding above the C-major chords of the piano and the orchestra. Dmitri usually shares the applause with his trumpeter.

He played the concerto for the first time at the opening of the Philharmonic on October 15, 1933 under the direction of Fritz Stiedry. At this concert Sonya sat in the thirteenth row — alone.

Another year of living with Nina and Dmitri was drawing to a close. Nadejda had not as yet been able to arrange to come to Russia, and, after a long correspondence with her sister, Sonya decided it might be better if she herself went to America. It would be easier for her to live far away from Dmitri, in another country. Meanwhile, Nina and Dmitri finally found a new apartment on Dmitrevsky Street, and Sonya was going there with them.

While Dmitri was playing his concerto in Kharkov, Sonya made the arrangements to move. "I was the last to leave Nikolaevskaya Street, which the children so loved — at eleven o'clock at night. The neighbors wept when they said good-by to me and I myself was terribly upset. From the exhaustion of moving, my thoughts were in a daze, but one thing was clear in my mind: that here had passed my life — so full in the last ten years of grief and misery — and that I could never start a new one. I wept as I said farewell to my 'cherry orchard.' "

Chapter

9.

"It takes more culture to recognize the value of this opera, than to reject it." — GOETHE (*in re* Mozart)

DMITRI SHOSTAKOVICH'S next work was his opera *Lady Macbeth of the Mzensk District.*[1] To the Western world, a confusing veil of mystery has fogged the significance of the events connected with it — events that almost wrecked the young composer's career.

It was Dmitri's long-cherished dream to compose a major work dealing with the freedom of the Russian woman. Russia never had an organized suffragette movement; it has always been the Russian men of letters who were responsible for their women's emancipation, beginning with Nekrassov's poem "Who Can Live Free and Happy in Russia?" written about the

---

[1] I wish to state here that my collaborator, Nadejda Galli-Shohat, is in no way connected either with the information I have received on the subject of Shostakovich's opera *Lady Macbeth* or with the treatment I have given it. After 1935 very few letters reached Mrs. Galli-Shohat from Russia, and the opera *Lady Macbeth* was not mentioned in these letters. My account is based on documents and reports published in the Soviet Union and available in this country. — V. S.

middle of the nineteenth century. Ostrovsky's Katerina in his play *Storm*, Dostoyevsky's Sonya Marmeladova in *Crime and Punishment* and his Grushinka in *The Brothers Karamazov*, Tolstoy's Katyusha Maslova in *Resurrection* and his *Anna Karenina*, the heroine of Chekhov's story *The Darling* — all were milestones in the history of this emancipation. The appearance of each of these characters caused great stir and interminable debates throughout Russia. In the case of Tolstoy's Katyusha Maslova, popular feeling ran so high that mock trials to determine her innocence or guilt were held year in and year out, with the cream of the Russian intelligentsia participating, and one was even held by the Russian immigrants in Paris as late as the early 1920's. Tolstoy himself challenged the greatest critics of Chekhov's *The Darling* and upheld the story as one of the most significant ever written on this subject.

"I want to write a Soviet *Ring of the Nibelung*," said Dmitri, in an interview with Leonid and Pyotr Tur. "This will be the first operatic tetralogy about women, of which *Lady Macbeth* will be the *Rheingold*. This will be followed by an opera written around the heroine of the People's Will Movement [Sofia Perofskaya, who organized the assassination of Alexander II, and was hanged with the rest of the ' First-of-March Men']. Then a woman of our century; and finally I will create our Soviet heroine, who will combine in her character the qualities of the woman of today and tomorrow —

from Larissa Reisner to the Dnieprostroy working-woman, Jennie Romanko. This theme is the leitmotive of my daily thought and will be for the next ten years."

It was not by chance that Dmitri chose this as his subject; who else among the Russian musicians of to-day has a comparable background — a background in which the women of the family played such a dominant role? He did not have to look far afield for his characters; there was his aunt Lyubochka, who had married her man in prison so that if need be she would be allowed to follow him into exile; there was his own paternal grandfather, sent to Siberia for hiding Kebalchich, who was a member of the People's Will Movement. Dmitri had intimate knowledge of the emotions of those who had lived through two revolutions, and this knowledge he had absorbed and made his own. And who could be a better subject for the "woman of our century" than his own mother? Dmitri's family provided him with a wealth of material to use — from the foresighted wisdom and gentleness of his grandfather, Vassily Kokaoulin, to the bravery and self-sacrifice of his sister Marusia.

Sonya had told her son the story of her family's trip through Siberia, of the tragic meetings with the convicts, and of the haunting songs the exiles sang on their weary march. And had Katyusha Maslova of Tolstoy's *Resurrection* been of flesh and blood, she might have met Sonya on her way to Siberia, for the Kokaoulins traveled the same road as did Tolstoy's heroine, and in the same year.

Dmitri wrote these convict scenes and their moving songs, which he had heard from Sonya, into the fourth act of his opera *Lady Macbeth*, and this act made a lasting impression on all who saw it.

For the first part of this noble task, Dmitri chose N. Leskov's novel *Lady Macbeth of the Mzensk District*, or *Katerina Ismailova* as it is frequently called, after the name of its heroine. He could not have chosen a more dramatic plot, with the completely corrupt society of the small town of 1840 as a background.

Katerina Ismailova, the wife of a rich merchant, tired of her dull and useless life, has, in the absence of her husband, taken as her lover a young clerk recently come to the household, by the name of Sergei. Sergei is caught and flogged by Katerina's father-in-law, a despotic, sensual old man. Katerina poisons the old man, and later with the help of Sergei strangles and kills her returned husband, who has confronted her with the story of her adultery. At her wedding to Sergei, they are arrested by the police, to whom they were denounced by the drunken servants who had discovered the body of their master while searching for wine in the cellar. The last scene is a convict station on the highway to Siberia, where the two lovers are among the criminals. Katerina is still in love with Sergei, who does not want her any more and uses her to get his new girl, who is one of the criminals in the transport. Katerina finds out, kills the girl and then herself, and the transport moves on.

In an article entitled "About My Opera," [2] which was published in the libretto, Dmitri wrote:

The opera *Lady Macbeth of the Mzensk District* was started at the end of 1930 and finished in December 1932. Why did I choose this particular subject for the opera? Because so far in the development of Soviet opera very little has been taken from our classical Russian literary heritage. And because Leskov's story is full of dramatic and social content. Perhaps there is not in the whole of Russian literature another work portraying the position of a Russian woman in the pre-revolutionary times more vividly.

I have treated *Lady Macbeth* on a different plan from Leskov. As one can see from the title, Leskov approaches the subject very ironically; the title indicates a tiny district where the heroes are small people, with much meaner and pettier interests and passions than the heroes of Shakespeare. Besides, Leskov, as a representative of pre-revolutionary literature, could not give the right treatment to the events that develop in his story.

Therefore my role as a Soviet composer consists in approaching the story critically and in treating the subject from the Soviet point of view, while keeping the strength of Leskov's original tale. Accordingly, I made some changes. If one remembers Leskov's story, Katerina Lvovna Ismailova commits three murders before she is sent into hard labor. (She kills her father-in-law, her husband, and her little nephew.) As my problem was to

---

[2] Entire article given in Appendix.

acquit Katerina Lvovna so that the spectator would be left with the impression of her as a sympathetic character, I omitted the murder of the nephew, which she committed for mercenary motives (so that she could receive the inheritance that would be left after the murder of her husband). I tried to treat Katerina as a character who would earn the sympathy of the listeners. To call forth this sympathy was not so simple: Katerina commits several acts that are not compatible with ethics and morality. Here is the basic point of difference from Leskov.

Leskov paints Katerina as a cruel woman, who is driven crazy by idleness and commits the murder of people who are innocent, according to Leskov. But I should like to explain these events in this way: Katerina is a clever woman, talented and interesting; owing to the hard and gloomy conditions of her life and to the cruel and greedy milieu of merchants that surrounds her, her existence becomes pitiful and uninteresting. She does not love her husband; she has no gaiety nor recreation of any kind. . .

I have tried to make the musical language of the opera very simple and expressive. I cannot agree with the theory, at one time very popular with us, that modern opera should not have any sustained vocal line, and that the vocal parts are nothing more than conversation in which the intonation should be marked. Opera, first of all, is a vocal composition; the singers should discharge their prime duty — to sing, not to talk or declaim or intone. Thus, all my vocal parts are built on a broad cantilena, taking into account all the possibilities for the human voice — that richest of instruments.

The music progresses always on a symphonic plan and in this respect the opera is not a repetition of the old operas which are built on separate numbers. The music flows without a break, being checked only at the end of an act; it is not built of small bits, but is developed on a grand symphonic pattern. This, of course, should be considered during the production of the opera, because every act except the fourth has several scenes, and those scenes are not designated mechanically by pauses, but by musical entr'actes, which allow time for the change of scenery. These musical entr'actes, which come between the second and the third, the fourth and the fifth, the sixth and the seventh, the seventh and the eighth scenes, are nothing but a continuation and development of the musical thought, and play a very important part in the exposition of what happens on the stage.

Dmitri's choice may have been partly due to his great admiration for Gogol, who, ninety-eight years before *Lady Macbeth*, unveiled before Russian audiences the corruption of the parasitic government officials in his masterly comedy *The Inspector General*. Gogol's play, whose purpose was to drag into the light "all that was bad in Russia" and hold it up to contempt, was a tremendous success — even in the spring of 1836 and in spite of the opposition attempted by the official classes, whose malpractices it exposed. Czar Nicholas I, on leaving the performance, is said to have remarked: "Everybody got it in the neck — and above all, I."

Mussorgsky also undoubtedly affected the young composer. Dmitri felt great reverence for his work and believes him the greatest of Russian composers. Mussorgsky's works *Boris Godunov* and *Khovanshchina* must have haunted Dmitri.

These two, Gogol and Mussorgsky, had obviously a powerful influence on him — a fact which can be clearly seen in the bitter sarcasm and terrific drama of his score of *Lady Macbeth*.

The opera was a success from the first. It played to packed houses in Leningrad, and was proudly presented in Moscow by the Nemirovich-Danchenko Theater, though Moscow liked it less than Leningrad. This Dmitri attributed to the fact that the Nemirovich-Danchenko Theater was famous for its stylized exaggerations and had not put on as good a production as had Leningrad. Dmitri was to play his piano concerto in Kharkov and he had gone straight there from the rehearsals in Moscow. His mind, however, was full of worries about the Moscow presentation of his opera. He told his friends: "If you want to see it, come to Leningrad and don't go to Moscow."

The Nemirovich-Danchenko Theater supplied its patrons with a handsomely bound libretto full of pictures of the production, and including ten articles in praise of the opera contributed by the members of the theater and a well-known critic. This critic, A. Ostretsov, in a detailed commentary on the music, wrote that only under the conditions of his country's historic revolutionary times could Shostakovich come forward as a critic of the old operatic clichés and traditions. With a sure hand, he wrote, Shostakovich "has torn off the masks and exposed the false and lying methods of the composers of bourgeois society. . . . Shostakovich brings off with success a new genre of tragic satire. His opera is a great victory and is the expression of the great creative upsurge that characterizes our musical front."

Nemirovich-Danchenko himself considered the opera "rich in dramatic, social, and psychological content"; the director stated that they "were witnessing the appearance of a most important work of art"; and the conductor reported: "It seems to me that *Katerina Ismailova* is truly the beginning of the Soviet *Ring of the Nibelung*."

Besides this fulsome praise at home, the opera was considered good enough to be exported to the United States of America. In addition to being a bona fide Soviet composer, Dmitri had now, for the first time, produced work worthy of being used as propaganda by his government. He was not unknown in America as a symphonic composer; in 1928 Leopold Stokowski had conducted the Philadelphia Orchestra in performances of his First Symphony and a few years later presented also the Third or "May Day" Symphony.

But *Lady Macbeth* was traveling in a different class. For in November 1933 the United States had formally recognized the Union of Soviet Socialist Republics. In April 1934 Amtorg, in its capacity as chamber of commerce, announced a "trade promotion tour" to sponsor a feeling of friendship between the two countries. The Soviet Ambassador, Troyanovsky, made a short speech on the radio, and the strains of the *Internationale* were heard for the first time over the air. *Lady Macbeth* was an integral part of this "campaign of Soviet-American understanding."

In July Lawrence Gilman wrote:

The American ambassador to Russia, William C. Bullitt, was quoted by this newspaper's Moscow correspondent, Mr. Ralph W. Barnes, as having declared, after witnessing both productions of "Lady Macbeth," that "this work should convince all doubters that opera may indeed be great art." It may perhaps occur to those who are not ambassadors that most "doubters" became convinced a good many years before Mr. Shostakovich was born "that opera may indeed be great art." But let that pass. Ambassadors are not expected to know much about Gluck and Mozart and Verdi and Wagner; and it is not necessary to boom Mr. Shostakovich's "Lady Macbeth of Mzensk" as an overwhelming disclosure of art and genius in order to convince inquisitive and open-minded opera goers that they should be on the look-out for this Soviet "Lady Macbeth." . . .[3]

Nor does one expect music-critics to understand much in politics. Mr. Gilman, bless his soul, seemed to overlook the fact completely that ambassadors do not, as a rule, "promote" musical compositions; that there must have been a good reason behind Ambassador Bullitt's having done just that in the case of *Lady Macbeth*. A champion of Russia since 1919, Mr. Bullitt no doubt saw clearly the purpose of sending the opera here — to stimulate the interest of Americans in the USSR.

[3] From the *New York Herald Tribune*, July 15, 1934.

Dr. Artur Rodzinski, who saw six performances of the opera in Russia, considered it a "sensational masterpiece and one of the most important contributions to contemporary music brought out in the past twenty-five years." He amassed an all-Russian cast and presented three performances of the opera in the United States in February 1935 — two in Cleveland and one at the Metropolitan Opera House in New York City. His production drew more comment than had any music to come out of Soviet Russia so far. The story of the opera became known during the early period of rehearsals through lectures and receptions, and a sold-out house greeted the performance; twenty minutes before curtain time a line of standees stretched for a block and a half from the box-office, and this in the snow and intense cold. "The raised-eyebrow brigade, who tolerate 'Tristan' after nine-thirty, turned out *en flamme* for its bitter bite into the Soviet's culture — most of them (an unheard of response by Metropolitan box-holders) at curtain time," said the *New York World-Telegram*.

The performances "fluttered the dowagers and disappointed the debutantes" in Philadelphia and brought an "SRO audience with standees by the dozens" in Cleveland — "an audience in bright array with color predominating . . . there was much red in the audience." The opera was undoubtedly successful, though the critics were divided in their opinions. Some thought that the writing was "scarcely up to permanent repertoire quality," that it was "melodrama of a rather juvenile sort"; others found it "rich in melodic content, poignant and expressive."

It was unfortunate that Shostakovich's noble idea of portraying the development of the freedom of Russian women was never sufficiently explained to the American public, and was drowned in the attitude of "Soviet composer gives hot stuff." The narrator who explained the opera between the acts, the comments printed in the programs, and the article appearing in the November issue of *Modern Music*, all failed to mention the composer's idea of the whole plan of the work — a work to which he was going to devote ten years of his life and thought.

* * *

The Shostakoviches had been living now on Dmitrevsky Street for almost two years. Dmitri's shortlived happiness had come to an end. In the beginning he and Nina had lived a gay life of parties, cars, and expensive restaurants, of which Sonya disapproved; but now they were seen in public less and less often together. Dmitri appeared either alone or with his friend Ivan Sollertinsky.

Nina was ill a great deal of the time and went away often for rest cures; either because they had not had any children, perhaps owing to Nina's present condition, or because they just couldn't get along, they had drifted apart. In the spring of 1935 Dmitri filed an

application for a divorce, "but nothing came of it."
Though Dmitri continued to spend most of his time
in Moscow, there was some sort of domestic recon-
ciliation and the idea of divorce was dropped.

While working on his opera, Dmitri completed his
Twenty-four Preludes for the Piano. These Twenty-
four Preludes are written one in the major and one in
the minor of each of the twelve keys. Dmitri composed
them all in Leningrad, mostly during 1933. These
short pieces were written sometimes one a day. Of the
twenty-four, the most popular are those with dancing
or marching tunes, very much in the style of Prokofiev.
The most impressive, however, is the fourteenth in
E-flat minor, which Leopold Stokowski has since orchestrated and of which he remarked: "So much is said
in such a short piece!" This somber composition contains passages that have the quality of a stirring call to
revolt and may have been inspired by the month in
which it was written — February. Dmitri's favorite
theme of the sour German band appears again in the
sixth prelude. The shortest of the twenty-four, number
twenty-two in G minor, is also one of the tenderest and
most moving.

From the frequent reports in *Sovietskaya Musica,*
one sees that Dmitri has taken a very active part in all
the forms that are a part of the growth of Soviet music.
He started a vigorous crusade for better musical criticism; he has always refused to listen to mere phraseology and disliked commonplace musical reviews

Letter of Dmitri to his Aunt Nadejda (1935).

11, IX, 1935, Leningrad

Darling Aunt Nadia,

Doctor Wieder came and brought your letter. Unfortunately, I couldn't talk to him, because he came without an interpreter and Mother was not at home. He speaks English and French, and badly (as I do) German. I didn't understand one thing, because he spoke to me of his friend who has invented some new system.

I will write more fully in a few days.　　　Your　　D. SHOSTAKOVICH

P.S.　Do you intend to come to the USSR?
　　My greetings to Jakov Alexandrovich.

explaining this or that page of music with the super-
ficiality of a mere program note.

In one of the reports on the Discussion of Soviet
Symphonism, he states his own attitude toward the
problem of pure and direct entertainment in music:
"Not that Soviets are always joyous or supposed to be.
But good music lifts and heartens and lightens people
for work and effort. . . . But I have almost never
heard that anyone has said that our Soviet symphony
should simply give pleasure (entertainment). Nevertheless, it is a serious problem that one should not dis-
miss. In the beginning, I agreed that I was guilty of
frivolity, using the street songs in my music. Perhaps
this was not right of me to do, but my intentions were
good. I wanted to write good and entertaining music
which would give pleasure to, or even just amuse, a
qualified listener." [4] By "qualified," Shostakovich undoubtedly means "musically educated." He goes on:
"And when an audience, during a performance of my
compositions laughs, or even smiles, it gives me great
satisfaction."

Dmitri was now making more money and he turned
the Dmitrevsky Street apartment over to his mother,
putting it in her name, and he and his wife moved into
spacious rooms in the Home of Soviet Composers.
Sonya had by this time become reconciled to the idea
of having a daughter-in-law; she had always thought
the trouble lay not so much in Nina, whom she con-

---

[4] *Sovietskaya Musica*, 1935.

sidered a girl of good character, but in the girl's up-bringing, which was foreign to Sonya's ideals and which she was afraid might be detrimental to her son's work.

Now that Sonya lived alone, she started giving piano lessons. Dmitri visited her every day, and by the end of the year he brought her the news that he and Nina were expecting a baby. Sonya was very pleased because, as she said, a child always brings happiness into a family. Dmitri himself was thrilled, and Sonya said: "He inherited that from me."

* * *

Lady Macbeth had been running for two years to packed houses when on the morning of January 28, 1936 lightning struck from a blue sky. *Pravda*, the organ of the Soviet government, carried an editorial under the title: "Confusion Instead of Music," with the subtitle: "About the Opera *Lady Macbeth of the District of Mzensk*." It ran as follows:

With the general cultural development of our country there grew also the necessity for good music. At no time and in no other place has the composer had a more appreciative audience. The people expect good songs, but also good instrumental works, and good operas.

Certain theaters are presenting to the new culturally mature Soviet public Shostakovich's opera *Lady Macbeth* as an innovation and an achievement. Musical criticism, always ready to serve, has praised the opera to the skies and given it resounding glory. The young composer, instead of hearing serious business-like criticism, which could have helped him in his future work, hears only enthusiastic compliments.

From the first minute, the listener is shocked by deliberate dissonance, by a confused stream of sounds. Snatches of melody, the beginnings of a musical phrase, are drowned, emerge again, and disappear in a grinding and squealing roar. To follow this "music" is most difficult; to remember it, impossible.

Thus it goes practically throughout the entire opera. The singing on the stage is replaced by shrieks. If the composer chances to come on the path of a clear and simple melody, then immediately, as though frightened at this misfortune, he throws himself back into a wilderness of musical chaos — in places becoming cacophony. The expression which the listener demands is supplanted by wild rhythm. Passion is here supposed to be expressed by musical noise. All this is not due to lack of talent, or to lack of ability to depict simple and strong emotions in music. Here is music turned deliberately inside out in order that nothing will be reminiscent of classical opera, or have anything in common with symphonic music or with simple and popular musical language accessible to all. This music is built on the basis of rejecting opera — the same basis on which "Leftist" art rejects in the theater simplicity, realism, clarity of image, and the unaffected spoken word — which carries into the theater and into music the most negative features of "Meyerholdism" infinitely multiplied. Here we have "Leftist" confusion instead of natural, human music. The power of good music to infect the masses has been sacrificed to a petty-bourgeois, "formalist" attempt to create originality through cheap clowning. It is a game of clever ingenuity that may end very badly.

The danger of this trend to Soviet music is clear. Leftist distortion in opera stems from the same source as the Leftist distortion in painting, poetry, teaching, and science. Petty-bourgeois "innovations" lead to a break with real art, real science, and real literature.

The author of *Lady Macbeth* was forced to borrow from jazz its nervous, convulsive, and spasmodic music in order to lend "passion" to his characters. While our music-critics swear by the name of socialist realism, the stage serves us, in Shostakovich's creation, the coarsest kind of naturalism. He reveals the merchants and the people monotonously and bestially. The predatory merchant woman who scrambles into possession of wealth through murder is pictured as some kind of "victim" of bourgeois society. The story of Leskov has been given a significance it does not possess.

And all this is coarse, primitive, and vulgar. The music quacks, grunts, and growls, and suffocates itself, in order to express the amatory scenes as naturalistically as possible. And "love" is smeared all over the opera in the most vulgar manner. The merchant's double bed occupies the central position on the stage. On it all "problems" are solved. In the same coarse, naturalistic style is shown the death from poisoning and the flogging — both practically on stage.

The composer apparently never considered the problem of what the Soviet audience expects and looks for in music. As though deliberately, he scribbles down his music, confusing all the sounds in such a way that his music would reach only the effete "formalists" who had lost their wholesome taste. He ignored the demand of

Soviet culture that all coarseness and wildness be abolished from every corner of Soviet life. Some critics call this glorification of merchants' lust a satire. But there is no question of satire here. The author has tried, with all the musical and dramatic means at his command, to arouse the sympathy of the spectators for the coarse and vulgar leanings and behavior of the merchant woman, Katerina Ismailova.

Lady Macbeth is having great success with bourgeois audiences abroad. Is it not because the opera is absolutely unpolitical and confusing that they praise it? Is it not explained by the fact that it tickles the perverted tastes of the bourgeoisie with its fidgety, screaming, neurotic music?

Our theaters have expended a great deal of labor on giving Shostakovich's opera a thorough presentation. The actors have shown exceptional talent in dominating the noise, the screaming, and the roar of the orchestra. With their dramatic action they tried to reinforce the weakness of melodic content. Unfortunately, this served only to bring out the opera's vulgar features more vividly. The talented acting earns gratitude; the wasted efforts, regrets.

A week later, in its issue of February 6, *Pravda* ran a second editorial, as prominently displayed as the first, entitled "Falsehood in Ballet." Written in the same vein as the first article, it denounced Shostakovich's ballet *The Limpid Stream* as being vulgar and stylized. It stated with resentment that the librettists and the composer had depicted the collective farmers of the Kuban region [5] as "painted peasants on the lid of a

---

[5] The Kuban region, in the northern part of the Caucasus, is inhabited chiefly by Cossacks.

candy-box." "The music is without character, it jingles, it means nothing. The composer apparently has only contempt for the national songs. . . . The authors of this ballet, the composer, and the producers apparently think that our public is not demanding, and will accept everything concocted by opportunists and high-handed men. In reality, it is only our music- and art-critics who are not discriminating. They will often praise undeserving works."

The confusion into which *Pravda's* editorials threw the musicians of the entire country, added to the discussions that took place in the Moscow and Leningrad Unions of Composers, would furnish material for a contemporary musical comedy — a modern *Meistersinger*. Streams of letters were written to the Composers' Unions, filled with vitriolic criticism of Shostakovich's work, and resolutions were published with the headlines: "Down with Bourgeois Æsthetes and Formalists"; "Long Live Music for the Millions"; "Down with Formalist Confusion in Art."

Before *Pravda's* editorials, any critical bickering would have been considered merely a sort of "domestic quarrel," not really significant no matter how important musicians thought it. But when the State stepped in, it became a different affair. The Moscow Union of Soviet Composers summoned all its members as well as critics and musicologists to a series of "creative discussions" to air their views. They were called to attend what should have been a fair trial, but what turned out to be a "hearing," since the verdict was already handed down. Dmitri Shostakovich was subjected to a court martial of his own, as his uncle Yanovitsky had been, but there was no Oscar Grusenberg to defend him. And it must be noted with regret that there was a lack of even elementary decency among the young composer's fellow musicians at this difficult time. Immediately after *Pravda's* editorials several orchestra conductors removed Dmitri's works from their programs and pianists asked to be excused from playing his piano concerto. The critic Ostretsov, a prominent musicologist who makes use of the most bewildering phraseology when he is not sure of his subject, asked the Moscow Union, on the day following *Pravda's* first editorial, to allow him to change the theme of his scheduled talk from *Lady Macbeth* to *Quiet Flows the Don.*

The sly Ostretsov knew which way the wind was blowing, for on the 20th of January, a week before the blow had fallen on *Lady Macbeth*, the Tass news bureau printed the following:

CONVERSATIONS OF COMRADES STALIN AND MOLOTOV WITH THE AUTHORS OF THE OPERATIC PRODUCTION "QUIET FLOWS THE DON"

On the 17th of January in Moscow the last guest performance was given by the Leningrad Academic Government's Little Opera Theater. Dzerjinsky's opera *Quiet Flows the Don* was played. Comrades Stalin and Molotov were present and also the secretary of the Central Committee of the USSR, Comrade Akulov, and the People's Commissar of Education, Comrade Bubnov. After the third act Comrades Stalin and Molotov had a talk with the authors of the opera, with composer I. Dzerjinsky, musical conductor S. A. Samosud, and theatrical director M. A. Terejkovich. During the conversation Comrades Stalin and Molotov gave positive appraisal to the work of the theater in the realm of the creation of Soviet opera, and remarked on the ideological and political value of the production of *Quiet Flows the Don.*

At the conclusion of the talk Comrades Stalin and Molotov expressed the necessity of remedying certain shortcomings in the production and expressed also their best wishes for further success in the work on Soviet opera.

For three days — February 10, 13, and 15 — the Moscow Composers' Union held sessions of heated denunciation of Shostakovich and his work, of those who were under his influence, and of those who they considered had influenced him. The hall could not accommodate all those who wanted to take part in the discussions, and the list of the men who had asked to be heard was not covered even after the three meetings. *Pravda's* editorials were taken as historical documents of unprecedented importance in the musical life of the Soviet Union, but the "creative discussions" have far more value as material; for in these speeches,[6] pleas, demands, and repentances are revealed not only the personal qualities of the speakers but the true state of affairs.

---

[6] Appearing in the publication *Sovietskaya Musica* for March 1936.

The leading tone in the discussions was set by *Pravda's* sentence: "All this is not due to lack of talent, or to lack of ability to depict simple and strong emotions in music." *Pravda* had thus made it clear that Shostakovich's talent was not to be attacked, but that all criticism should be leveled at his tendencies, which were definitely in the wrong direction, tendencies which were labeled as "formalistic."

This most elastic of terms came into general use in 1932, when the Central Committee of the Communist Party advocated more self-criticism. Everything and anything could become "formalistic" and the critics who were to guide not only the public but also the artists never knew which way to turn. This fateful word hung now over the heads of the men who tried their best to preserve their positions by keeping their opinions in accord with *Pravda's* and repenting their past mistakes. In his opening speech, Cheliapov, the president of the union, explained that the term "formalistic" was to be understood thus: "Every composition should be considered formalistic in which the composer fundamentally does not have as his aim the presenting of new social meanings, but focuses his interest only on inventing new combinations of sounds that have not been done before. Formalism is the sacrifice of the ideological and emotional content of a musical composition to the search for new tricks in the realm of musical elements — rhythm, timbre, harmonic combinations, etc."

"This is only a general definition," explains Chelia-pov (unfortunately), "which must be fitted to each individual composition."

The musicians were at first split into three groups: one said there was no necessity for change — they would go on as they had, with Shostakovich as their leader; the second group, who were rivals of the young composer, wanted to go on without Shostakovich; and the third, and largest, group said: "Let's live as we did, but without formalism as the head of our musical front." But during these discussions in Moscow the musicians gradually presented a united front against the young composer; they all seem to have taken *Pravda's* words as the only light in their dark and confused minds, were all repentant of their sins, blamed the critics for everything, and gave Dmitri a thorough kicking around. They emphasized again and again that the editorials in *Pravda* expressed "the attitude of the working class toward art," that they were documents on "the question of politics in art which have come from the party."

Emotions ran high during these debates. In the confusion the speakers brought up subjects that had no relation to Shostakovich and, in a frenzy of self-criticism, denounced everything and even turned on one another. "In no other country," cried one of them, "do composers brag so much as in the Soviet Union. And yet we can only count two or three symphonies, practically no piano compositions, and still very little music for singers." This statement brought a roar of protest. The names of Shostakovich and Prokofiev were repeatedly pronounced as the ones who were responsible for all evils — "Shostakovich, who was heralded as the leading figure among our composers, and about whom there was more propaganda than any other, both here and abroad. We have a whole line of little Shostakoviches — composers and critics!" As for Prokofiev, who had had a tremendous influence on young Soviet composers, had he not made the statement last year that he writes two kinds of music — "one for the masses, and the other — Was it perhaps for posterity?"

Tikhon Khrennikov, a well-known composer whose works have been heard in America, declared indignantly that Prokofiev considered Soviet music provincial and that the most contemporary Soviet composer was Shostakovich. "This," said Khrennikov, "created a confusion in the minds of the young composers. On the one side was the desire to write simple music for the masses — and on the other was the musical authority of Prokofiev. In these difficult times we received guidance neither from the critics nor from our union. The critics wrote rhapsodic odes to Shostakovich. The only ones who helped were the teachers. I told Miaskovsky that Prokofiev considered Soviet music provincial. 'Pay no attention to it,' he replied."

Neuhaus, director of the Moscow Conservatory, spoke very mildly, and mostly of things that had no relation to the question at hand; he mentioned Gorky and the pleasure he had had in talking to Romain Rolland. As for Shostakovich, he thought that after *Pravda's* editorial the young composer should be grateful and happy. Neuhaus was also present at a performance of *Lady Macbeth*, but "was bored and left after the second act."

"The difference," he stated, "between the *Lady Macbeth* of Leskov and the *Lady Macbeth* of Shostakovich is great. Leskov's story is written with the heart's blood; one can feel that the man was shaken by a terrific vision, and from this comes its tremendous power, the force of the language, the poetical images. This is awe-inspiring tragedy. With Shostakovich this is all lost; it is lost on account of skepticism and in some places even cynicism. Cynicism should not be tolerated in art."

Neuhaus was slightly mixed up, however; although *Pravda* reported itself as being deeply touched by his heart-rending speech, *Lady Macbeth* was later removed from the list of Leskov's works in the Soviet *Encyclopedia* — for it was Leskov and not Shostakovich who was considered the reactionary.[7]

While these heated arguments were proceeding, *Pravda* clarified its position by laying the blame on the critics: "The editorials of *Pravda* have caught off guard

---

[7] *Lady Macbeth of Mzensk* is listed as one of Shostakovich's major works, but there is no mention of it under Leskov's name. This is due to the fact that the compilation of the encyclopedia took five years and the article on Shostakovich was written in 1933; by 1938 Leskov had lost his *Lady Macbeth*.

the masked defenders of decayed bourgeois music. This is the reason for the bewilderment and the anger of these men. The idolater of this trend which disfigured Shostakovich's music, the untiring troubadour of Leftist distortion, Sollertinsky, correctly appraised the situation when he declared at the session of Leningrad music-critics that there is nothing more for him to do in Soviet musical art and that he will terminate his 'activities.' The mask is torn off! Sollertinsky speaks his own language."

The word "troubadour" was picked up immediately by the speakers at the union, and the composers, who before this had "walked with their fists in their pockets," now lit openly on the critics for all they were worth.

In the summing up, Cheliapov pointed out that "certain of our composers have based their ideas on the criticism that they received from the West about our music. To our disgrace, some bourgeois critics gave a more correct appraisal of the work of our composers than did our own critics. A Prague paper, which is sympathetic to us, commenting on the cello sonata of Shostakovich after its presentation in Prague, said that it is a model of bourgeois music. And our critics never mentioned one word of this. It should not be forgotten that, among the Western critics, there are some who sympathize with us, some who are indifferent, and some who are direct enemies. But to consider that Western criticism is the rule by which we should measure our own Soviet works is to turn everything inside out."

Part of the warmth of Moscow's criticism came no doubt from the traditional feud that existed between the musicians of the two capitals. As for Leningrad, whose Composers' Union held meetings at the same time as those in Moscow, its musicians stood by Shostakovich's talent and shared the blame equally with him. They also took the words of *Pravda* as infallible wisdom, they also blamed the critics Sollertinsky and Rabinovich, and the conductor Samosud, who had stated: "There has not been, in the last fifty years, a composition that can be compared to *Lady Macbeth*." But instead of condemning Shostakovich, the Leningrad musicians pledged themselves to help the young composer realize his mistakes and to set him on the right path.

But there was not one who had the courage to come out against *Pravda's* editorials or to say that the whole affair, as the union had handled it, was a disgrace — and that the arguments about "formalism" were incoherent nonsense. Even the young composer's teacher, Maximilian Steinberg, side-stepped: "When Shostakovich came to me with his *Aphorisms* (1927), which were an expression of the new trend Shostakovich was taking under Sollertinsky's influence, I told him that I could not understand them — that they were foreign to me. After this, he did not come to see me any more."

And, finally, his best friend Ivan Sollertinsky, publicly washed his hands of the whole thing. In a long speech, delivered in his best oratorical style — a speech including the names and the works of countless old and modern composers, together with philosophers, historians, æstheticians — Sollertinsky "repented his sins." He steered away from the main issue and avoided Shostakovich's name as much as possible; but he did rip apart the opera *The Nose*, which he had so highly praised before, and linked Shostakovich with Meyerhold, whose name was already in disgrace. He finished his speech by apologizing for his earlier statement that he was through with Soviet music and by saying that he needed time to reconstruct his position and that now "I have decided to study the musical folklore, among which will be the folklore of the Caucasus, and am now studying for this purpose the Georgian language." (Joseph Stalin is a native of Georgia.)

The only musician who did not express his views in this whirlwind of comment and criticism, was Dmitri Shostakovich. The publication *Sovietskaya Musica*, which carried all of these debates, has not printed a single statement by Shostakovich — if he made one. Furthermore, in the list of Dmitri's works, which he himself recently compiled for Nicolas Slonimsky [8] — a list in which the composer marked with asterisks the works which he thinks are unrepresentative of his pres-

---

[8] List given in Appendix.

ent ideals in music — *Lady Macbeth* and *The Limpid Stream* stand unmarked, as do the rest of his works which were so violently torn apart during those debates.

*   *   *

"Break it up, break it up! There's nothing to see!"

IT is interesting to note that no one expressed publicly the fact that *Pravda's* editorials went far deeper than mere music criticism. In its issue of February 13 *Pravda* said: "It is with surprise that we note that the *Literary Journal* treated the editorials of *Pravda* as an affair apart from literature, and even uninteresting. The paper has not carried one word of comment. Apparently that happy journal considers that its little home is perched off on the side-lines. Oh, holy simplicity! In the same blissful state of ignorance are also the other newspapers. *Izvestia* is silent. The usually energetic *Comsomolnaya Pravda* is in the same position! Is it possible that these papers have nothing to say?"

Even this significant statement did not call forth any response, and yet the musicians of Russia had before them a parallel in their own history — in the experience of Anton Rubinstein with his opera *The Merchant Kalashnikov*, in 1889. The description of this by Catherine Drinker Bowen, in her book *Free Artist*, is so similar in many respects to the case of *Lady Macbeth* that it is worth quoting in full:

This was the fateful opera that had been withdrawn nine years ago after one performance which, unluckily, had taken place on the very day a Nihilist was hung in Petersburg — far too significant an analogy with the Merchant who also met his fate at the hands of a Tsar. Latterly, however, Alexander III had commanded a revival of the opera which he had been told was truly Russian. It was his firm policy to patronize Russian art. After all, no Nihilists had been hung lately. What this monarch considered the firm policies of his reign were succeeding admirably; the country was comparatively quiet.

Arrangements went forward and then, a few days before the dress rehearsal, Rubinstein received a letter from the directorship of the opera house, informing him the *Merchant* was again withdrawn "for political reasons." This, said Rubinstein grimly, was opera-house politics, not national politics. Indignant and powerful friends went straight to the Tsar. Faction ran high; Prince Obolensky was enthusiastic in the opera's defense, the Counts Lamsdorf and Hirz professed themselves "shocked" by the rehearsal they had seen. And then the Procurator himself, Professor Pobyedonostsev, took a hand. In all good faith he attended the dress rehearsal — and emerged, he reported to his sovereign, "as if stunned." Horrible vice, corruption and violence were depicted on a stage decorated like a church with ikons — even haloed ikons. Songs set to the words of the holy Psalms were sung to motifs recognizable as church music! Above all, Tsar Ivan, a monster of a creature, indulged in an orgy of drinking right there in the holy place. "I write these lines at night, after the theatre. Let your Majesty believe me — coming out of the box I saw two people with tears in their eyes and heard them say: 'My God, why do they show such a scene?' Above all, why show it now, when Russia is just beginning to live again, when every eye is turned toward our Tsar and finds, at last, ideal traits that our people have so ardently, passionately desired in their ruler? The first time Kalashnikoff was performed, in 1880, things were quite different in our country; it was a time of madness, irritation, of great sedition. But now! Even if the Tsar and Tsarina, in the simplicity and purity of their hearts, see no offense, we Russians, we the people, are offended by that scene which reviles all that we hold saintly." [9]

The story was current in Moscow that when Stalin finally saw *Lady Macbeth* he did not like it, that he walked out before it was over, and that this took place a few days before *Pravda's* bombshell. European as well as American critics and public were shocked by this high-handed attitude, and puzzled over it. Obviously, it could be seen that there was nothing bourgeois about the story, for it paints the merchant middle class of the nineteenth century in most unfavorable colors. And both the text and the music clearly point up the scoffing by the downtrodden servants at their masters. The monumental symphonic music pictures the drab atmosphere and the moral sufferings of the oppressed, and draws the idle and corrupt existence of the merchant class with bitter sarcasm and irony, especially in the scene of the marital quarrel, one of the most strik-

---

[9] From Catherine Drinker Bowen's *Free Artist, the Story of Anton and Nicholas Rubinstein* (New York: Random House; 1939), by permission of Catherine Drinker Bowen.

ing life-scenes found in the opera literature of the world.

The average American, whose conceptions of art and music are radically different from those of the Soviet Union, would be apt to react to *Pravda's* editorials in the words of Hamlet: "Buzz, buzz!" "Formalistic ideas, founded on bourgeois conceptions," would make no sense to him. As for the "concessions to bourgeois taste," there is the danger that the same American would say: "It tastes pretty good to me." And only confronted with the "cheap and unsoviet," might he say: "Well, you have me there, brother, you ought to know." It is obvious that such an attitude, taken by a Russian of, say, less popularity than Shostakovich, could land him in a climate far cooler than he was accustomed to; and even a man of Shostakovich's name and position could find himself relegated to comparative oblivion by the complete suppression of his work.

The two editorials could hardly have been prompted by one man's reaction, no matter how high this man's position might be. Stalin's personal displeasure had about the same amount of influence as Lenin's enthusiasm for Beethoven's Appassionata Sonata had in fostering the popularity of that composer. The mere fact that *Pravda* took a hand in it showed that the matter was of far more importance than mere criticism of a musical score, which, after all, could be revised, modified, improved, or cut. *Pravda's* interest in the affair signified that it was of vital importance to the State itself, for *Pravda* is a political organ that does not as a rule review musical events.

Dmitri Shostakovich had always believed that Soviet music was closely bound up with the life of the country. The bitter proof that he was right came when his own work fell beneath the pressure of events on his own State.

Soviet Russia had been uneasily watching the spread of fascism and the complete failure of the European powers to stop its aggression. It was aware also that all was not as it should be on the home front. As early as 1933 Stalin had spoken of Communist blunders, of their failure to foresee the methods of hostile forces boring from within. Collectivization was facing great difficulties in collecting the vital seed supplies which the peasants were hiding. Constant sabotage and deliberate looting brought about finally the death penalty for those actively hindering the spring planting. "Stern methods" were to be used against the Cossacks who resisted collectivization.

Then, on December 1, 1934, Kirov, a high official of the Leningrad Soviet and a close friend of Stalin, was assassinated, and a wave of suspicion and fear of treason swept the country. The official communiqués reported that a conspiracy had been discovered within the Communist Party ranks in Leningrad to assassinate all of the Soviet leaders simultaneously. The following day the workers demanded the punishment of the traitors. Thousands of arrests were made and about four hundred suicides were reported within the next few days.

According to the verbatim reports of the trials (which were held two years later), published in English by the People's Commissariat of Justice of the USSR, in Moscow in 1936–8, a most fantastic plot to wrest the power from the Soviet leaders by killing them had been in process of preparation for the last few years by members of the Communist Party in high official positions, under the direction of Trotsky, who was in exile.

The government explained, in the words of the accused men, how the conspirators, who had accomplices in all the key positions in industry and communications, as well as in the Kremlin itself, had sabotaged and "wrecked" the country during the early 1930's. To achieve their final success, they had planned their country's defeat in the event of war. Germany was to attack Russia, which, after the work of sabotage had been thoroughly accomplished, would have been unable to put through any mobilization. In the meantime groups of terrorists had been assigned the tasks of "removing" the present heads of the government.

The arrests of about fifty of the most prominent members of the Communist Party — men whom the Russian people had known as the leaders of the great Revolution and therefore had always regarded as above suspicion — confused and frightened the populace. Men in the streets became suspicious of one another, and distorted rumors shattered the confidence of a whole nation. The Russian people avoided any contact with foreigners and even refrained from correspondence with friends outside of Russia. Foreign musicians were informed that their contracts would not be renewed and it was politely suggested that they leave the country when their work was done.

"Let's fight with gentle words Till time lend friends and friends their helpful swords"; [10] this was the attitude of the European powers toward the growing fascist menace. But Soviet Russia had to rely on her own strength, for whom could she call friend in 1935? The government realized that a thorough job of housecleaning had to be done and done quickly. And the place to start was the home front.

One has only to remember the years that followed the Revolution to realize that the task of welding the home front into a strong and self-confident body was not so simple. There was a time when marriages and divorces were practically non-existent. If a man lived openly with a woman for some time, she was considered by the State as his wife, and it did not matter if he was not meticulous enough to register with the marriage bureau. Even if he was married with the greatest pomp that the State could provide, and then in three days decided that he had had enough of matrimony,

---

[10] From Shakespeare's *Richard II*.

he could casually drop a postcard in the mailbox stating his desire for a divorce, and thereby automatically terminate his marriage and relieve himself legally of all responsibilities. The housing problem, which threw more than one family into one crowded communal apartment, presented an unlimited field for free love and adultery, and a lack of moral standards as we know them in the Western world.

Antagonism within the family was prompted by the government's encouragement of the young generation's criticism of the old. This criticism by children of their parents, accompanied at times even by denunciation based on theories of "party lines," produced most disastrous consequences. Nihilism — disregard of authority — created fertile soil for this extreme split in family relations, as well as complete disrespect for parental authority, called *"Bazarovschina"* (from Turgenev's *Father and Son*). One must also take into consideration that in any new revolutionary country youth has the upper hand, youth born and brought up on the streets during the revolution and civil war, with only the "order of the day" as the moral guide.

In addition, by 1932–3 the government, proud of its accomplishments, was urging increasing self-criticism and freedom of expression. Even the famous GPU (the secret police) was dissolved.

But with the assassination of Kirov and the switch from a Marxist to a national policy, all this came to an end. Lectures, discussions, newspapers, but, even more, theaters, music, and moving pictures are the tools that a government can use to strengthen and even, when it is necessary, reverse the attitude of its people. And this the Soviet Union proceeded to do.

The threat of a brutal foreign invasion apparently loomed closer by the hour and there was no time to lose in getting ready to meet it. The first and most important part of the task was already begun — with the arrests — and that was to eradicate the most gigantic Fifth Column the world has ever known, if the reports of the confessions, which came out later, were true. The authenticity of the reports may still have to be established for the historian, but the fact remains that the Kremlin treated them as established facts and acted accordingly.

It was imperative, in any case, to rebuild the self-confidence and the solidarity of the Russian people. The love of children for their parents and for their homes, which they were to defend as precious possessions and not regard merely as another place provided by the government where they might rest their heads, sexual relationship as the fundamental bond between two people — these had to be restored to their former rights and respect — bourgeois or not bourgeois. And, finally, love for their "rodina" — a proud name for fatherland — this was the spirit which the government of the USSR had now to build up for the attacking nations to face — and dare them to destroy it.

While calling the citizens to their duties as patriots,

whipping up their fervor with the spirit of "my country, right or wrong," the Soviet government could not afford to have in the people's favorite theaters plays that depicted the Russian character with criticism and sarcasm, leaving the audiences in gloom and pessimism. The building up of self-confidence, even though it might be based on undue optimism, was of the utmost importance in order to avoid any sense of inferiority.

Shostakovich's opera *Lady Macbeth* left its audiences in deep gloom. It had not a single note of optimism in it from beginning to end. All of the Russian characters in the opera, from the peasants to the merchants, were depicted as base and immoral and, in view of the new policy, Shostakovich had even failed to make a noble character of his heroine.

What the country needed was a heroic subject, one that was close to the memories and the lives of the people. Michael Sholokhov's novel *And Quiet Flows the Don*, which in scope reminds one of Tolstoy's *War and Peace*, fulfilled the demands. Sholokhov dedicated his book to "The Socialist Village," and in it he describes the life of the Don Cossacks before the first World War, during it, and through the Revolution. The traditional Cossack heroism has been built up in the minds of every Russian into a legend, as representing the strength and the backbone of the Russian army, whether Czarist or Red. However, the Cossacks as a unit, always true to their origin, have never cared to take orders from Moscow, and the Soviet government tried very unsuccessfully to disband them and mix them with the rest of the class of Russian peasant workers.

By 1934, when Shostakovich wrote *The Limpid Stream*, the Soviet government had ordered "stern measures" to be used against them whenever they resisted. In Shostakovich's ballet, therefore, the Cossacks of the Kuban region were not depicted in their own tribal dress nor singing and dancing any of their own folk-songs. But now, in 1936, when the co-operation of the Cossacks was becoming increasingly necessary and they had to be re-established as a military unit, they were given back the right to wear their glamorous uniforms and to stand separate from the peasantry. Therefore it was most opportune that Dzerjinsky had written an opera based on Sholokhov's novel, which was appearing in serial form in *Pravda*.

Although this opera was far below the caliber of Shostakovich's music, it was immediately brought before the public, for it was more in the character of Cossack folklore, closer to the soil, and fulfilled far better the needs of the time. The final touch to the affair of *Lady Macbeth* was the awarding of the Stalin Prize to Dzerjinsky's opera — an opera dedicated to Shostakovich and written, as Dzerjinsky clearly emphasized during the Leningrad discussions, with Shostakovich's most co-operative help.

As early as January 11, 1936 Soviet Premier Molotov quoted from *Mein Kampf* Germany's expansion aims at the expense of the Soviet Union. Again in February the Soviet press quoted from the same book, pointing out Hitler's intentions toward France. The Soviet government knew that war was inevitable, and the opening gun in the campaign on the home front was the "banning" of *Lady Macbeth*. *Pravda's* editorials, blasting the opera, coincided neatly, with only a few weeks to spare, with the Nazi march into the Rhineland — the first blow of the Wehrmacht against the Treaty of Versailles.

Chapter

10.

"He's all the mother's from the top to toe."
— SHAKESPEARE

ALTHOUGH *Pravda's* editorials were not an official ban on Dmitri's music and, according to Nicolas Slonimsky, *Lady Macbeth* remained in the repertoire of some companies, comments on the young composer's work ceased to appear and there is no mention of his name in *Sovietskaya Musica* for the rest of the year 1936, nor during 1937, except for a few belated slaps in the form of bad reviews from abroad, which normally would never have been reprinted. For those musicians in the far-flung corners of the Soviet Union who received their news through *Sovietskaya Musica*, Dmitri Shostakovich ceased to exist. There was even no obituary notice by Ostretsov, and as for Sollertinsky, he was too busy studying the Georgian language.

But Dmitri was not Sonya's son for nothing. He kept his feelings about the affair to himself. His Fourth Symphony, which was already in its tenth rehearsal under the baton of Fritz Stiedry, he withdrew before performance and it has never been played in public. It was a long work, lasting fifty minutes, gloomy and introspective, and there was no point in pouring oil on the fire. Dmitri returned to his duties as professor at the Conservatory, where he had been teaching for the last year, and quietly started work on his Fifth Symphony. His only happiness at this time came from the fact that in the spring of 1936 he became the proud father of a little daughter, Galya.

Dmitri's Fifth Symphony was first performed at the Festival of Soviet Music in Leningrad on November 21, 1937, an occasion marking the twentieth anniversary of the October Revolution. Harold Denny, the correspondent of the *New York Times*, sent a special wireless dispatch with headlines that read:

COMPOSER REGAINS HIS PLACE IN SOVIET

Dmitri Shostakovich, who fell from grace two years ago, on the way to rehabilitation. His new symphony hailed. Audience cheers as Leningrad Philharmonic presents work.

The Fifth Symphony opens what is becoming known as "the second period" in Dmitri's music. Its first movement is Shostakovich at his best — lyrical and sober, with a broad sweep to the melodic line — and shows a new maturity; this maturity reaches its greatest depth and power in the third movement, the now famous Largo. The entire symphony seems, indeed, to satisfy the demand of the Soviet people that their new music be "powerful and intelligible." The symphony was played three times to packed houses, with the tickets sold out hours before the performances; *Pravda* beamed on the young composer and spoke of the "grandiose vistas of the tragically tense Fifth Symphony with its philosophical search." Dmitri's triumph could be compared only with the comeback of an idol of the prize-ring, and was just as dramatic as his downfall, for the public was no more prepared for this sudden acclaim that it had been for *Pravda's* bolt from the blue a year and a half before.

There had been some changes in Russia during those eighteen months. The trials of the "anti-Soviet bloc of Rightists and Trotskyites" were still being held, but at the same time a new constitution was being planned by Stalin and was discussed eagerly throughout the country. The Russians considered it the greatest expression of freedom and the rights of men in the history of mankind. Many prominent musicians commented on it and perhaps the one coming from Prokofiev had a direct influence on the fate of Dmitri's music, for though Prokofiev had been branded as a "formalist" during the *Macbeth* discussions, the power of his influence and his authority could not be disregarded.

The new constitution, said Prokofiev, was an act of great faith in the Soviet citizen. There was no better way to lift the morale of a human being than to give him one's confidence. He did not doubt that the new constitution would help to foster further universal lib-

*After a Moscow performance of the Fifth Symphony in 1938.
Left to right, first row: People's Artist of the USSR, V. Nemirovich-Danchenko; People's Artist of the USSR, A. Goldenvaizer;
composer Dmitri Shostakovich; Honoured Artist of the USSR,
A. Gouk; and standing next to him, extreme right, People's Artist
of the USSR, S. Samosud. (Photograph by Sovfoto.)*

*Dmitri working on Mayakovsky's comedy, " The Bedbug," for the
Meyerhold Theater in Moscow in 1929. Left to right: Dmitri (at
the piano); Meyerhold (seated); and Mayakovsky (standing left).*

eration of the Soviet conscience from the ideologically bad and outlived past.

"It is no secret to anyone that we do not always do our work correctly, and that we do not always respect our own word and are not sufficiently eager to raise the standard of our qualifications. . . ."

The points at the end of his sentence suggest that Prokofiev had more to say on the subject; but what he did say was sufficient to remind his colleagues to be open-minded in their appraisals, and, once they had recognized the worth of a work, to stick by their criticism of it.

Since the *Lady Macbeth* affair musicians had cautiously avoided all association with Dmitri. But Prokofiev's praise of the young composer and *Pravda's* words about his talent were not forgotten. The government valued his musical ability and the road had always remained open to him to re-establish himself by producing a work which would meet with the government's approval. Such was the Fifth Symphony.

In 1938 Dmitri wrote a string quartet; he had written very little chamber music so far: a Trio for violin, cello, and piano in 1923, which remained in manuscript; two pieces for string octet in 1925; and a Sonata for cello and piano in 1934. The Soviet critics called this new quartet (opus 49) a "lyrical intermezzo"; in four simple and conventional movements, it is almost classical in style. It is light-hearted in mood and very unpretentious.

In 1938, Dmitri started work on a new symphony. In a statement about it he said: "I have set myself a task fraught with great responsibility, to express through the medium of sound the immortal image of Lenin as a great son of the Russian people and a great leader and teacher of the masses. I have received numerous letters from all corners of the Soviet Union with regard to my future symphony." [1] This symphony, Dmitri's Sixth, was presented at the Moscow Festival of Soviet Music in 1939, but Lenin's name was not connected with it. The Sixth, like the Fifth, had no political program attached to it; these two works stood purely on their musical merit. The Sixth Symphony is in three movements and is full of the spirit of joy and energy; Dmitri had not, however, been able to live up to his Fifth, and the Sixth was received less warmly.

In the summer of 1940 Dmitri wrote his Piano Quintet. The quintet was given its first performance at the Moscow Festival of Soviet Music on November 23 of that year, with Dmitri at the piano. It had the kind of instantaneous success that would not be unusual in the case of a showy concerto or a brilliant symphony, but which was surprising for a chamber-music composition. It is an exquisitely written piece which surpasses any of the composer's piano works. It is in four movements, with the first consisting of a prelude and fugue written in what might be called a Bach-Shostakovich style, which soon becomes far more

---

[1] *Sovietskoye Iskusstvo*, November 1938.

Shostakovich than Bach. The fugue is academic, but is far from reaching the austere grandeur of the great master of the fugue. The most brilliant of the movements is the scherzo, written in the style of Beethoven, but with an unmistakable Russian quality of harmony and with the mocking gaiety that is so typical of Shostakovich. The finale is definitely ballet music, with a march rhythm; one of its themes is the traditional tune that announces the coming of the clowns in Russian circuses — a tune that the composer cleverly introduces in inverted form.

Dmitri won the Stalin Prize of one hundred thousand rubles for his Piano Quintet; this prize was given by the government in recognition of signal achievements in the arts and sciences and is the largest sum of money ever paid for one piece in the history of music. *Pravda* called the quintet "lyrically lucid, human and simple"; *Pravda* now seems to comment on all of Dmitri's achievements, which is an exceptional honor.

Encouraged by his growing success, Dmitri decided that the time had come for him to attempt once more the creation of a monumental Lenin Symphony. In December 1940 he stated: "In 1941 I hope to complete my Seventh Symphony, which I shall dedicate to the great genius of mankind — Vladimir Ilyich Lenin." But Fate, who had doomed his *Lady Macbeth*, gave him this time a far greater dedication for his new work.

On the morning of June 22, 1941, German bombers swooped over Russian cities and the Nazis began their march on Moscow. Dmitri was on his way to the stadium to see a football game when he heard Molotov's radio address, announcing the sudden attack. Dmitri reported:

I volunteered for service at the front, and received the reply: "You will be called when required." So I went back to my duties at the Leningrad Conservatory. We attended recitals by members of the graduating class, gave an evaluation of their performances, and signed their diplomas. This year, many gifted pianists, violinists and singers graduated from the Leningrad Conservatory.

I joined the conservatory fire-fighting brigade. We were housed in barracks and it was here that I began work on my Seventh Symphony. Later I was asked to become musical director of the Popular Guard Theater. Soon this theater became the center of Leningrad's leading playwrights, poets and writers. We produced several interesting plays, one of them an operetta on how Ribbentrop gathered his celebrated conference of diplomats shortly after the outbreak of the war. One after the other, groups of actors from our theater left for the front. And when some of them returned they brought with them the splendid fighting spirit of our army. I visited front-line units on two occasions and witnessed numerous instances of the courage that typifies our people. Simple people, men you meet every day, turn out to be real heroes.

Take, for example, Danya Shafran, member of the Popular Guard, who saw some very heavy fighting and showed distinguished valor. One of my pupils, Fleischman, who has just finished his first one-act opera, was always very modest and inconspicuous in the conservatory. But now in these trying days he proved worthy of his country. And my Seventh Symphony (I am working on it now) will tell of these so-called simple people.

The first part of the symphony tells of the happy, peaceful life of a people confident in themselves and in their future. It is a simple life, such as was enjoyed by thousands of Leningrad's Popular Guards, by the whole city, and the whole country before the war broke out. Then comes the war. I have made no attempt at naturalistic interpretation of the war by imitating the booms of cannon, shell, explosions, etc. I tried to give an emotional image of the war. The reprise is a memorial march, or more correctly a requiem for the war victims. Plain people pay tribute to the memory of their heroes. The requiem is followed by an even more tragic theme. I don't know how to describe it. Perhaps it is the tears of a mother, or even that feeling which comes when sorrow is so great that there are no more tears. These two lyrical fragments form the conclusion of the first part of the symphony. The closing chords resemble the din of distant battle, a reminder that the war continues.

While I was working on this music, Leningrad was converted into an impregnable fortress. Fresh Popular Guard detachments were constantly being formed. The entire population learned the art of warfare and it seemed that war had replaced all other affairs. I found, however, that that was not so, for one of my friends told me that all tickets for the Philharmonic concerts had been sold. Indeed at all these concerts I found the audience in high spirits and keenly responsive to our performance. My ex-

citement at these concerts was something new, for I came
to understand that music, as every art, is a genuine re-
quirement of man.

My work on the symphony continued at a rapid pace.
I finished the second and third parts in a surprisingly
short space of time. Generally speaking, I do not like to
hurry with my work, but on this symphony I worked with
a speed that I myself couldn't understand. When I am
through with it, I will have to start from the beginning,
of course, for it still requires much polishing and work
over details. But as I was writing the score, I didn't think
of this aspect. The second and third parts of the symphony aren't closely bound to the main theme. They serve
as a lyrical relief. The second part of the symphony is a
lyrical scherzo. The third part, adagio, is the dramatic
center of the symphony.

It is with a feeling of admiration and pride that I watch
the heroic deeds of Leningrad's people. Despite frequent
air-raid alarms, everyone goes about his work with pre-
cision and efficiency. People are calm and life continues
normally. Factories and offices successfully cope with the
rush orders. Theaters are as active as ever and give the
people that spiritual encouragement which helps them in
their work at the front or rear. Everyone shares the common cause and strives for a common aim. Wives and
mothers don't complain. They show every concern for the
men-folk at the front and they themselves help to guard
the city and fight fires. Even children are doing their bit
to help strengthen Leningrad's defenses.

I have still to write the finale of the symphony, but its
general outlines are already clear to me. I could describe
it with one word — *victory*. This finale is devoted to a
happy life in the future after the enemy will be crushed.

Never have I dedicated any of my works. But this symphony, if my work meets with success, I intend to dedicate to Leningrad. Every note in it, everything I have put into it is linked up with my native city, with these historic days of its defense against the fascist barbarians.[2]

Dmitri stayed in Leningrad for three months after the outbreak of the war, three months during which he worked on his symphony whenever he had time to spare from the many duties he had taken on. He had an unusual capacity for concentration, and had always been able to work no matter what went on around him, as long as it was not shouting or singing. This capacity stood him now in good stead. "Even during air raids," relates his wife, Nina, "he seldom stopped working. If things began getting too hot, he calmly finished the bar he was writing, waited until the page dried, neatly arranged what he had written, and took it down with him into the bomb-shelter. Whenever he was away from home during an air-raid alarm, he always phoned me asking me not to forget to take his manuscripts down into the shelter."

In October Dmitri, who had stubbornly refused to leave his city of Leningrad, was finally told by the government to move with his family to Kuibyshev. Besides little Galya, Nina and Dmitri now had a three-year-old son, Maxim. Both children were blue-eyed and fair-haired like their father. They were not yet being taught

---

[2] Cabled dispatch which appeared in the *New Masses*, October 28, 1941.

music, but they could both sing correctly many tunes from Dmitri's compositions. Their favorite one at the time was the theme of the first movement of the new symphony. "They often beg their father to play for them," says Nina, "and they climb onto the lid of the grand piano and sit as quiet as mice, all ears."

While the Germans were hammering at the gates of Moscow and Hitler was announcing to the world that the Russians had been crushed, never to rise again, Dmitri was writing the last pages of his symphony — the symphony about the horrors of war, of the ruthless foe that was strong — but not strong enough to break the spirit of the people who were willing to fight and to die for their ideals and their country. He finished it in December and it was put immediately into rehearsal under the baton of Samosud, with Dmitri attending every rehearsal, and sometimes not only Dmitri but his children as well. "There they sat in the director's box," says Nina, "and when Professor Samosud, the conductor, asked them: 'What have you come to listen to?' they replied: 'Our symphony.' But in the middle of the first movement Maxim suddenly started 'conducting' with such desperate energy that he had to be taken home."

"During the time of rehearsals," relates Ilya Slonim, sculptor, and son-in-law of Ambassador Litvinov, "he seemed in high spirits, but the day for the first public performance was a terrible ordeal for him. He was in and out of our apartment (we were next-door neighbors) all day, never staying longer than ten minutes, looking even paler than usual and, almost stammering, imploring us not to go to the concert, hoping all his friends would stay away, and the next moment calling up the theater and begging for 'just one more ticket,' for a girl in the post-office who had asked him to get her in.

"He seemed to suffer agonies during that first performance. The audience insisted on seeing him before it began, and he stood up on the platform, rigid and unsmiling. And when, after it was over, there were enthusiastic clamors for the composer, the grim young man once more climbed up to the platform, looking as if he were going to be hanged."

Here, for the second time in the twenty years of her son's public life, Sonya is mentioned in an interview about Dmitri.

"Another thing that is realized as one comes to know Shostakovich better," writes Mr. Slonim, "is the influence of his mother. I appreciated him still more after I got to know her — a beautiful old woman, with kindly, blue Russian eyes. They have much in common — the son is strikingly like his mother and they share many interests. Mrs. Shostakovich, senior, is an able musician herself, and was his first teacher. She is very proud of her son and modest about herself. When not talking about her Dmitri, she is talking of Leningrad." [3]

So Sonya is still by the side of her son in Kuibyshev;

---

[3] Reprinted by courtesy of Vogue, September 1, 1942.

she has lived to see the fulfillment of the dreams she had never once lost sight of during the long hard years on Nikolaevskaya Street. She has been with Dmitri in his greatest triumph and has heard him speak for Russia to the whole world.

APPENDIX

THE SHOSTAKOVICH FAMILY

DMITRI BOLESLAVOVICH SHOSTAKOVICH, father of the composer, was born in Narim, Siberia; his parents were political exiles. He had three brothers and two sisters. His father, Boleslav Petrovich Shostakovich, whose ancestors were Lithuanians, was active in the insurrection in Poland in 1863–4, and later was arrested for hiding Nikolai Ivanovich Kebalchich, a revolutionary long sought by the authorities and later hanged with the famous "First of March Men." After the assassination of Alexander II, Boleslav Petrovich Shostakovich was exiled to Narim, Siberia, along with the rest of the men implicated in the death of the Czar. Narim had become an exiles' camp after the Polish Insurrection of 1863, when several score of them were sent there.

The maiden name of the composer's grandmother was Varvara Shaposhnikov.

Dmitri's brother, Boris Boleslavovich Shostakovich, was a navy officer, but was lost without trace after the first World War. There were rumors of his having gone to America and some faint trails even led to Chicago and Manila, but beyond that nothing was ever known. Dmitri's older brother, Vladimir, lived all his life in Siberia, but little was known of him.

His sister Marusia married Maxim Lavrentyevich Kostrykin, then a student of engineering at the Mining Institute of St. Petersburg. He was of peasant stock, a social revolutionist, and was involved in one of the student movements. He was arrested and sent to Siberia.

245

Marusia became a doctor of medicine. The Shostakovich family later spent much time scheming to get Kostrykin back from Siberia. They finally procured a passport for him, and while they were planning how to get it to him, he suddenly appeared at their apartment. He returned to his work at the Institute, where all the professors knew him, and continued his brilliant studies under the assumed name in his new passport. He also lived once again with his wife and children; but since he was under a different name, and Maxim Kostrykin was, to all intents and purposes, still in Siberia, Marusia, in the eyes of the government, was living in sin.

THE KOKAOULIN FAMILY

THE origin of the family name of Kokaoulin was discovered by the composer's uncle, Jakov Vassilievich Kokaoulin, in the small Siberian town of Kirensk, over 650 miles north of Irkutsk. There still stands in Kirensk an old black church, built of wood with windows of mica, dating back to the earliest days of the Russian Orthodox Church in Siberia. In its archives Kokaoulin found documents concerning a group of Greek monks and priests who, in 1518, were invited by Prince Vassily III to come to Moscow and correct the translations of the sacred writings and books of the Greek Orthodox Church. The group was headed by Maxim Grek — Maxim the Greek — who became one of the most remarkable writers and educators in Russian history.

Maxim Grek was born of a prominent, educated, and cultured family some time around 1475 in Arta, in Albania. He received his education in Italy and became a devoted pupil of Savonarola, the famous Florentine churchman. In Russia, Maxim threw the whole weight of his authority and knowledge into the fight against the high priesthood of the Russian Orthodox Church and exposed the corruption and vice in which the priests and monks lived. He fought the existing economic situation and finally even criticized the divorce and the second marriage of Prince Vassily III.

By this act he brought upon himself the anger of the Prince, and in 1525 he and his Greek followers were judged by the high court of the Orthodox Church and were found guilty of incorrect and false translations of the church books. They were exiled to Volokolamsk Monastery, thirteen miles from the town of Volokolamsk in Moscow County. One of Maxim's men, whose nickname was Kakosbules (κακοσβουλης), meaning in Greek "Bad Counselor" or "Evil Adviser," appears in the archives of the church at Kirensk, which contains the complete account of Maxim's punishment and exile. The name Kakosbules was corrupted into the Russian version Kakosvulin (какосвулин), owing to the Russian habit, lasting to the end of the nineteenth century, of pronouncing *v* for the Greek *b*. Eventually the two middle consonants were dropped (како[св]улин) and the name became Kokaoulin.

The family did not like the sound of the first syllable and so changed the *a* to *o*. The nearest English approximation to the Russian sound of the name is given in the spelling used throughout this book, with each syllable pronounced separately: ко-кa-оу́(oo)-лin.

[All of the Kokaoulin family papers and documents remain in the possession of Ivan Petrovich Zakonov, the husband of Vera Kokaoulin, in Omsk.]

ABOUT MY OPERA

By Dmitri Shostakovich

THE opera *Lady Macbeth of the Mzensk District* was begun at the end of 1930 and finished in December 1932. Why did I choose this particular subject for the opera? Because so far in the development of Soviet opera very little has been taken from our classical Russian literary heritage. And because Leskov's story is full of dramatic and social content. Perhaps there is not in the whole of Russian literature another work portraying the position of a Russian woman in the pre-revolutionary times more vividly.

I have treated *Lady Macbeth* on a different plan from Leskov. As one can see from the title, Leskov approaches the subject very ironically; the title indicates a tiny district where the heroes are small people, with far meaner and pettier interests and passions than the heroes of Shakespeare. Besides, Leskov, as a representative of pre-revolutionary literature, could not give the right treatment to the events that develop in his story.

Therefore my role as a Soviet composer consists in approaching the story critically and in treating the subject from the Soviet point of view, while keeping the strength of Leskov's original tale. Accordingly, I made some changes. If one remembers Leskov's story, Katerina Lvovna Ismailova commits three murders before she is sent into hard labor. (She kills her father-in-law, her husband, and her little nephew.) As my problem was to acquit Katerina Lvovna so that the spectator would be

249

left with the impression of her as a sympathetic character, I omitted the murder of the nephew, which she committed for mercenary motives (so that she could receive the inheritance that would be left after the murder of her husband). I tried to treat Katerina as a character who would earn the sympathy of the listeners. To call forth this sympathy was not so simple: Katerina commits several acts that are not compatible with ethics and morality. Here is the basic point of difference from Leskov.

Leskov paints Katerina as a cruel woman, who is driven crazy by idleness and commits the murder of people who are innocent, according to Leskov. But I should like to explain these events in this way: Katerina is a clever woman, talented and interesting; owing to the hard and gloomy conditions of her life and to the cruel and greedy milieu of merchants that surrounds her, her existence becomes pitiful and uninteresting. She does not love her husband, she has no gaiety nor recreation of any kind. But there suddenly appears Sergei, whom Katerina's husband, Zinovy Borisovich, has engaged as clerk. This is what happens: She falls in love with Sergei, who is a negative and unworthy character, and in her love for him she finds happiness and a purpose in life. In order to make Sergei her own, she commits several crimes. When Boris Timofeyevich, her father-in-law, catches Sergei after a rendezvous with Katerina and gives orders to have him flogged, a desire for revenge awakens in her. She poisons her father-in-law for the tortures inflicted on her lover. When, later, Sergei confesses to her that he does not want to be her secret lover, that he dreams of becoming her husband, Katerina answers that it will be done. And so when her husband returns from a long trip, she and Sergei strangle him so as to remove every obstacle to their plans. It would take a lengthy explanation for me to describe how I justify these acts — this is better accomplished by the musical material, which I consider plays the leading and decisive part in an operatic work.

Katerina, in her love for Sergei, sacrifices herself completely. Besides Sergei, nothing exists for her. When, after the discovery of her crimes, she is sent into hard labor with Sergei and is convinced that he has left her for the prisoner Sonyetka, Katerina goes through terrible physical suffering and finally drowns Sonyetka in the river. Then she drowns herself because life without Sergei's love has lost its interest for her.

I have tried to make the musical language of the opera very simple and expressive. I cannot agree with the theory, at one time very popular with us, that modern opera should not have any sustained vocal line, and that the vocal parts are nothing more than conversation in which the intonation should be marked. Opera, first of all, is a vocal composition; the singers should discharge their prime duty — to sing, not to talk or declaim or intone. Thus, all my vocal parts are built on a broad cantilena, taking into account all the possibilities for the human voice — that richest of instruments.

The music progresses always on a symphonic plan and in this respect the opera is not a repetition of the old operas which are built on separate numbers. The music flows without a break, being checked only at the end of an act; it is not built of small bits, but is developed on a grand symphonic pattern. This, of course, should be considered during the production of the opera, because every act except the fourth has several scenes, and those scenes are not designated mechanically by pauses, but by musical entr'actes, which allow time for the change of scenery.

These musical entr'actes, which come between the second and the third, the fourth and the fifth, the sixth and the seventh, and the seventh and the eighth scenes, are nothing but a continuation and development of the musical thought, and play a very important part in the exposition of what happens on the stage.

A few words about the chief characters and their musical characterization: The chief character in the opera is Katerina Lvovna Ismailova (dramatic soprano). Her musical language — her musical image — stems completely from my idea that she must appear sympathetic. She has a great deal of soft, warm lyricism, sincere and infinite grief, and much joy in her happy moments. All of her music has as its purpose the justification of her crimes. Speaking in the language of Dobrolyubov, one might say that she is "the ray of light in a dark kingdom." There is no other hero or positive character in the opera. All of the others, Boris Timofeyevich, Zinovy Borisovich, Sergei the clerk — all are the products of the dark and hopeless merchant life of that time. The clerks of the merchants Ismailov are potentially the merchants of the future — like the Ismailovs, they lie and short-change so that later they may open their own little shops and become merchants. Therefore I characterize these as negative.

The suffering people of this epoch — an epoch built on exploitation — is shown in the fourth act, at "hard labor." There is no darker picture of the old times than Russian hard labor, than the way-stations for the broken-down people who moved under guard into the far expanses of the former Russian Empire — to penal servitude. An absolutely just reaction — though perhaps unconscious — was that of the peasants who considered the "hard labor" exiles not as criminals, but as children of misfortune. Let us remember the picture from the *Memoirs from the House of the Dead* by Dostoyevsky, where he describes how a little girl gave a kopeck to him, who was a prisoner at hard labor, and how in the villages the peasants gave a roll or a few pennies to the unfortunate ones. I felt such emotion toward the hard laborers when I composed the fourth act of this opera — they inevitably call forth this sympathy.

Sergei, the clerk: He represents, so to speak, the evil genius appearing in Katerina's life when it was sad and dark. He is a petty scoundrel whose object in life is to achieve wealth and "to satiate himself with the sweetness of a woman's body," as he says. He meets the beautiful Katerina and would like to "taste" her; it is flattering to him that the gentlewoman pays attention to him. On account of him, she kills her father-in-law and her husband — all for him. And when Katerina, from being a wealthy woman, becomes a hard laborer, he, without a thought, leaves her and finds a more interesting subject for himself in the prisoner Sonyetka. Sergei is a clerk who has picked up here and there a little "culture," who reads little books, and who speaks in a refined and affected manner — all, of course, with a lackey's point of view.

The music strips Sergei, so to speak, naked. It was my problem as a composer to lay bare the inner workings of every character. The lyrics of Sergei are insincere and theatrical; his sufferings are all pretense. Through his air of slick haberdasher oozes the future kulak who, if he had not been sentenced to hard labor, would have become a merchant exploiter. He is no Don Juan in the sense of the famous legend — no conqueror of women's hearts. Not only is he not a Don Juan, but he is a cruel and hideous criminal who, cleverly using his handsome exterior, bewitches Katerina. Only the accidental exposing of the crime prevents him from becoming a rich merchant — and he goes to hard labor. But even there he shows himself still petty and vulgar.

Boris Timofeyevich, the father-in-law of Katerina, is a strong and husky old man — a typical master kulak, who would not stop at anything to achieve his ends — bad-tempered and mean. He never speaks to Katerina without shouting at her.

His son, Zinovy Borisovich, Katerina's husband, is a moron born of a healthy father. It must be pointed out that Boris Timofeyevich is a strong and healthy man — even probably a clever one, who enjoys authority and power in his own milieu; Zinovy Borisovich, on the contrary, is a pitiful man and more like the frog who tried to blow himself up to the size of a bull. According to the musical characterization, one can see that Zinovy tries to bully and show his power, but he cannot outdo his father; and it often happens that he begins to talk very swaggeringly and tries to prove that he is the boss in his own house — but the music exposes him and allows us to see the petty moron, the product of the merchant class. Though he is, according to law, the master of all the wealth of the Ismailovs, the real master is Boris Timofeyevich.

These two men who are so close to Katerina must be exposed in every way. This is done by musical means. For instance, when Zinovy returns from his long journey and finds Katerina with Sergei, one gets the impression that he will deal severely with them. Therefore his entrance is preceded by fanfares which give the idea that something terrible will happen; but the horror comes from another quarter. Katerina gets into an argument with Zinovy and he increasingly loses his head; when he tries to show his power as a husband, he meets his end. Katerina, with the help of Sergei, kills him.

The secondary characters also play an important role in the opera. For instance, the priest, Sonyetka, the old hard-labor criminal, and the ragged peasant. This last is a typical Russian drunkard with no moral principles, who is sometimes on the side of Katerina and sometimes against her.

The problem of the actors is complicated and difficult: A fine voice without the power of creating a character on the stage will mean nothing. This power is necessary to "put over" the opera to the listeners. The chorus is also very important; it should not be merely static, as it so often is in other operas, but should play an active role. All of its members should sing and act well and move about the stage freely, participating in all the action.

In conclusion, a few words about the musical character of the opera: As I said before, the opera is written on a symphonic pattern from the first to the last note. In connection with this, the importance of the orchestra increases — it does not accompany but it plays perhaps an even more important part than the soloists and the chorus. The conductor of the opera should find, therefore, the golden mean, so as neither to subdue the orchestra nor to cover the singers.

LIST OF WORKS BY DMITRI SHOSTAKOVICH

(From "Dmitri Dmitrievitch Shostakovitch," by Nicolas Slonimsky [1])

THIS list was compiled by Shostakovich for the writer of this article.[2] Works marked with asterisks have been repudiated by the composer as unrepresentative of his present ideals in music.

Opus

1. Scherzo in F-sharp minor for orchestra (1919). *MS.

2. Eight Preludes for piano (1919–20). *MS.

3. Theme with Variations for orchestra (1920–2). *MS.

4. (1) *The Grasshopper and the Ant;* (2) *The Jackass and the Nightingale,* for voice and orchestra, text by Krylov (1922). *MS.

5. *Three Fantastic Dances* for piano (1922). Published by the Music Section of the State Publishing House, 1926.

6. Suite for Two Pianos (1922). *MS.

7. Scherzo in E-flat major for orchestra (1923). *MS.

8. Trio for piano, violin, and cello (1923). *MS.

9. (1) Fantasy; (2) Prelude; (3) Scherzo for cello and piano (1923–4). *MS.

---

[1] *Musical Quarterly,* Vol. XXVIII, No. 4. Reprinted by permission.

[2] The opus numbers of this list differ from those in the printed edition of some of the early works.

10. Symphony No. 1 in F minor (1924–5). Published by the Music Section of the State Publishing House, 1926. First performance, Leningrad, May 12, 1926.

11. Two pieces for string octet (1925): (1) Prelude; (2) Scherzo. Published by the Music Section of the State Publishing House, 1927.

12. Sonata for piano (1926). Published by the Music Section of the State Publishing House, 1927.

13. *Aphorisms* (ten pieces for piano). Published by Triton, Leningrad, 1928.

14. Symphony No. 2, Dedication to October (1927). Published by the Music Section of the State Publishing House, 1927. First performance, Leningrad, November 6, 1927.

15. *The Nose*, opera in three acts after Gogol (1927–8). Lithographed. First performance, Leningrad, January 13, 1930.

16. *Tahiti-Trot* (orchestral transcription, 1928). MS. lost.

17. Two Pieces by Scarlatti for a wood-wind ensemble (orchestral transcription, 1928). MS. lost.

18. Music for the film *The New Babylon* (1928–9). MS.

19. Incidental music to Mayakovsky's comedy *The Bedbug* (1929). MS.

20. Symphony No. 3, May First. Published by the Music Section of the State Publishing House, 1932. First performance, Leningrad, November 6, 1930.

21. Six Songs to words by Japanese poets, for voice and orchestra. (1) *Love*; (2) *Before the Suicide*; (3) *Immodest Glance*; (4) *For the First and Last Time*; (5) *Love*; (6) *Death*. *MS.

22. *The Golden Age,* ballet in three acts (1929–30). A suite from this ballet was published by the Music Section of the State Publishing House in 1934. First performance, Leningrad, October 27, 1930.

23. Two pieces for orchestra (1929): (1) Entr'acte; (2) Finale. *MS.

24. Music to Bezimensky's comedy *The Shot* (1929). MS.

25. Music to the drama by Gorbenko and Lvov *The Virgin Soil* (1930). MS.

26. Music to the film *Alone* (1930). MS.

27. *Bolt,* ballet in three acts (1930–1). First performance, Leningrad, April 8, 1931. MS.

28. Music to Piotrovsky's play *Rule Britannia* (1931). MS.

29. *Lady Macbeth of the District of Mzensk,* opera in four acts (1930–2). Piano score published by the Music Section of the State Publishing House, 1935. First performance, Leningrad, January 22, 1934.

30. Music to the film *Golden Mountains.* A suite from this music published by the Music Section of the State Publishing House, 1935.

31. Music to the play *Conditionally Killed,* by Voevodin and Riss (1931). MS.

32. Music to *Hamlet* (1931–2). MS.

33. Music to the film *Passer-by* (1932). MS.

34. Twenty-four Preludes for piano (1932–3). Published by the Music Section of the State Publishing House, 1933.

35. Concerto for piano and orchestra (1933). Published by the Music Section of the State Publishing House,

1934. First performance, with composer at the piano, Leningrad, October 15, 1933.

36. Music to the film *Tale of a Priest and his Dumb Hired-Man* (1934). MS.

37. Music to *The Human Comedy*, after Balzac (1933–4). MS.

38. Suite for jazz orchestra (1934): (1) Waltz; (2) Polka; (3) Blues. First performance, Leningrad, November 28, 1938. MS.

39. Ballet, *The Sparkling Brook*, in three acts (1934). First performance, Leningrad, June 4, 1935. MS.

40. Sonata for cello and piano (1934). Published by Triton, Leningrad, 1935.

41. Music to the film *Girl Companions* (1934). MS.

42. Five Fragments for orchestra (1935). *MS.

43. Symphony No. 4 (1935–6). Put in rehearsal by the Leningrad Philharmonic in December 1936, but withdrawn by the composer. *MS.

44. Music to Afinogenov's play *Salute to Spain* (1936). MS.

45. Music to the film *Maxim's Return* (1936–7). MS.

46. Four Songs to Pushkin's texts (1936). MS.

47. Symphony No. 5 (1937). Published by the Music Section of the State Publishing House, 1939. First performance, Leningrad, November 21, 1937.

48. Music to the film *The Days of Volotchaevo* (1936–7). MS.

49. String Quartet (1938). Published by the Leningrad Music Section of the State Publishing House, 1940. First performance, Leningrad, October 10, 1938.

50. Music to the film *Vyborg District* (1938). MS.

51. Music to the film *Friends* (1938). MS.
52. Music to the film *A Great Citizen,* first series (1938). MS.
53. Music to the film *The Man with a Gun* (1938). MS.
54. Symphony No. 6 (1939). Published by the Music Section of the State Publishing House, 1941. First performance, Moscow, December 3, 1939.
55. Music to the film *A Great Citizen,* second series (1939). MS.
56. Music to the film *Silly Little Mouse* (1939). MS.
57. Quintet for piano and string quartet (1940). Published by the Union of Soviet Composers, 1941. First performance, Moscow, November 23, 1940.
58. Orchestration of Mussorgsky's opera *Boris Godunov* (1940). MS.
59. Symphony No. 7 (1941–2). First performance, Kuibishev, March 1, 1942. First American performance, NBC orchestra, Arturo Toscanini conducting, July 19, 1942. MS.

INDEX

i

INDEX

iii

INDEX